GREAT CHEFS
INTERNATIONAL

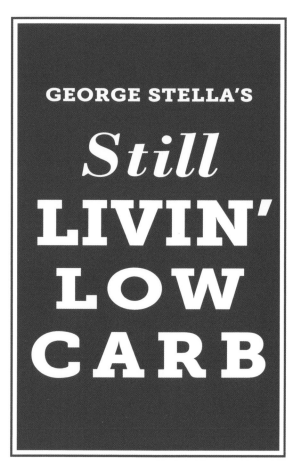

GEORGE STELLA'S
Still LIVIN' LOW CARB

GEORGE STELLA
with CHRISTIAN STELLA

A Lifetime of Low Carb Recipes

Published by Pretty Food Press, LLC and Great Chefs International

www.prettyfood.com
www.greatchefsinternational.com

First paperback edition 2012

Authors:
George Stella
with Christian Stella

Book Design and Food Photography by
Christian and Elise Stella

Copy Editing by
Kelly Machamer

This book is not meant to dispense medical advice. Please consult your
doctor before making any dramatic changes to the way you eat.

Nutritional analysis provided on each recipe is meant only as a reference and has been
compiled to the best of our ability using nutritional analysis software. Due to differences
in sizes, brands, and types of ingredients, your calculations may vary. Calories in this
book were rounded to the nearest 5 and all other amounts the nearest .5 of a gram.

ISBN 978-0-9846682-0-5

Printed in the USA

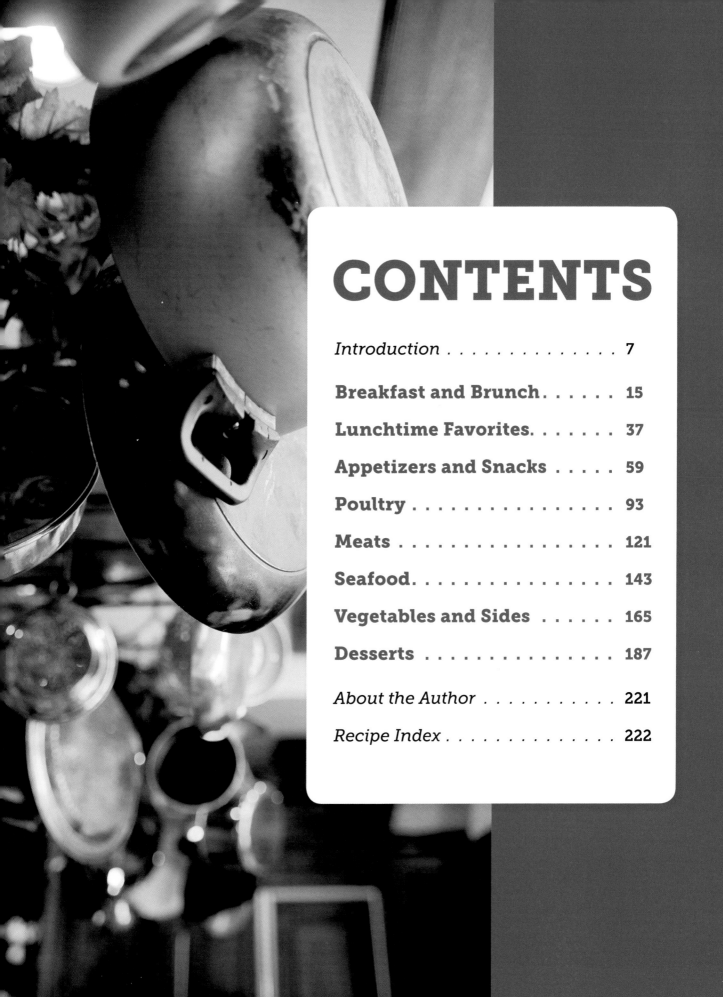

CONTENTS

INTRODUCTION

It has been nearly a decade since the publication of my first cookbook, Livin' Low Carb, and even I couldn't have imagined how important that book would become. To this day, it is still one of the bestselling books on low carb cooking, and for many, it set the standard for eating on a low carb lifestyle.

When I sat down to compile this, my fifth cookbook, I decided to go back to the basics and back to what resonated so well with the readers of my first book. I decided to write a cookbook that was the best representation of how my family ate while we were losing weight and to improve upon many of my classic techniques using all that we've learned in the last decade. I set out to write not only a cookbook but also a book that could teach you my low carb cooking techniques to use in your own recipes.

The title, Still Livin' Low Carb, isn't meant to imply that this is merely a follow-up to that first cookbook. Instead, it's meant as a sort-of shout from the rooftops that we're still here— my family—we're still living a low carb lifestyle and we've kept the weight off for 10 years doing it. Many believed that low carb was simply a passing fad, but the continued interest in my books and recipes have proven otherwise. Many believed that you couldn't keep the weight off with low carb, but we've done it, and we're still doing it.

The only thing that has changed since we first began our low carb lifestyle is the widespread acceptance that white, refined carbohydrates are simply not good for you. Ten years ago, there was a lot of opposition to this idea, but today you'd be hard pressed to find anyone that doesn't watch or want to watch their consumption of white carbs in some way or another. Beyond that, it seems that study after study on the low carb lifestyle have shown more and more positive results — not just for weight loss but also for cholesterol levels and other important contributors to overall health.

But I am not a doctor; I'm a chef and I've always been one—I just haven't always been the way I am today.

My name is George Stella and more than a dozen years ago I weighed 467 pounds. I was confined to a wheelchair, destitute, and destined to die. I had severe sleep apnea and I stopped breathing countless times each night. I had congestive heart failure and doctors

had made it clear that if I didn't lose weight, I would die. My heart could not supply blood to a person of my size and it was only a matter of time. I was not even forty years old.

My family had followed down my path and it seemed that we had all given up. My wife Rachel, who had never had a weight problem previously, had resigned to the fact that we had become a fat family and put on most of her extra weight in only a few short years. My son Anthony was up and down over the years, eventually bordering on obese by the time he hit high school. But worst of all, my son Christian had been obese since the age of 4. With severe asthma, Christian was in and out of hospitals his entire life, and by the age of 15 he weighed over 305 pounds. He was not just on his way to following in my footsteps, he already was. By the time he reached

middle school, we had to pull Christian out of public school to get him away from an onslaught of bullying.

I've told this story many times now and it doesn't get any less real. I don't get any less detached from it. While I sometimes worry that I am repeating myself, I feel that other than my skills in the kitchen, my family's story is the most important thing I have to share. We were at the absolute bottom of it all and we came back. I feel it is so imperative to let others know that they can come back. No matter how bad the situation and no matter how overweight or how unhealthy you are—you can overcome. We overcame. We did it. We're still doing it. Every year is another notch on the belt for us and we know a thing or two about drilling extra notches into our belts!

The change for us came when we heard about low carb diets, specifically Dr. Atkins' diet. With me facing certain death and my family following suit, we were willing to try anything. Rachel read Dr. Atkins' book from cover to cover, as my sleep apnea had me dozing off far too often to read anything. She wasn't convinced low carb would work—none of us were—but we decided to try it anyway.

What came next changed our entire lives. My family lost over 550 pounds in less than three years! What started as something we thought we'd give one month turned into a way of life that we continue to follow to this very day. Against all odds, I am very much alive and 265 pounds slimmer. Rachel and Anthony each lost 75 pounds and Christian dropped 160 pounds—more than half his body weight.

The weight loss allowed me to get out of the wheelchair and back into restaurant kitchens cooking in prestigious restaurants such as Victoria and Alberts at Walt Disney World. My sleep apnea disappeared and my heart is still ticking. Then it got my whole family on TV as poster children of the low carb "craze." (I say "craze" because, for us, it's just a way of life!) Eventually I had my own show on the Food Network, Low Carb and Lovin' It.

The concept of low carb eating is simplest when put in these terms: Our body can burn carbohydrates or fat to get energy; however, it prefers carbohydrates. When given an ample supply of carbohydrates, it burns those to fuel our body and converts any remaining carbohydrates to fat that it then stores in case it doesn't get carbohydrates in the future. This causes you to gain weight. Now, if you do not supply your body with carbohydrates, a switch clicks and your body begins burning fat for fuel full-time—this fat-burning state is known as "ketosis," and being in ketosis causes you to *lose* weight.

It is hard for most people to understand how you can eat things like cream cheese or heavy

cream and still lose weight, but I assure you that my family did. It is because our bodies, due to eating naturally low carb food, were in ketosis and burning fat. This is also the reason why I must stress that "cheating" on a low carb lifestyle when you still have a lot of weight to lose is very counter-productive. Binging on carbohydrates can cause your body to fall out of the fat-burning ketosis state for several days, causing you to go back to storing the fat that you eat.

I must stress again that I am not a doctor, but I have done my best to explain how a low carb lifestyle works in the way that I understand it. For more detailed information on ketosis, I implore you to pick up a book by Dr. Atkins. This information can, and does,

We reinvented all of our favorite comfort foods so that we would never go without. We would have been happy to simply be healthy, but thanks to low carb, we feel like we are living out a dream. We can only hope that you will share in our love of good, fresh food. And if you ever need support, we'll still be here.

For more information on our weight loss, living a low carb lifestyle, and to participate in an active support community, please visit:

www.StellaStyle.com

fill an entire book and, as a chef, my book is a cookbook first and foremost.

The most important thing you need to know is that all of the foods in the recipes in this book were regularly eaten by my family as we lost weight. We never actually counted carbohydrates, but instead we chose to simply purchase and eat only fresh foods that were naturally low in carbohydrates all of the time. If you keep your kitchen stocked with these foods and eat dishes like those in the recipes in this book, there simply is no reason to count anything. Though we've included the nutritional information for each recipe in this book, we care far more about the ingredients than the numbers.

Living a low carb lifestyle shouldn't be hard work and it definitely shouldn't be boring. I've spent years perfecting the recipes in this book to ensure that my family stuck with it.

OUR LOW CARB PANTRY

We use a variety of healthier alternatives to keep our recipes free of white carbs like sugar and all-purpose flour. We purchase all of these ingredients at our local grocery stores and you should not find anything in this book that isn't easily available—you just need to know where to look! As some of these ingredients may sound foreign to you at first, I will do my best to explain why we use them and how they can be found.

Almond Flour

Almond flour is such an important substitute for white flour in our baked goods (especially desserts) that we have included a recipe to make your own on page 213. It couldn't be any easier to make and you should always have some on hand. We like to keep it fresh by keeping it in an airtight container in the freezer. It is extremely important to note that while almonds do contain fat, this fat is the good (monounsaturated) kind, and should definitely not be frowned upon. Many of the dessert recipes in this book may look like they contain a high amount of fat because of this, but this good fat is exactly the thing that leaves you full and satisfied on a low carb lifestyle. Store-bought almond flour does exist, but it can be hard to find, expensive, and not as fresh as homemade.

Soy Flour

We also use soy flour as a high-protein substitute for white flour in some baked goods (especially savory ones). Soy flour can achieve a lighter, fluffier texture that rises better than almond flour. You can usually find soy flour in the baking aisle or organic and

natural foods section of your ordinary grocery store. Bob's Red Mill, Arrowhead Mills, and Hodgson Mill are the most readily available brands. While soy flour will always be best in the recipes that use it, if you have a soy allergy, almond flour can be substituted.

Milled Flax Seed

Milled Flax Seed will usually be available near the soy flour in the baking aisle or natural foods section of your grocery store. What you are looking for is ground flax seeds that resemble coarse wheat flour, not whole flax seeds. Hodgson Mill calls this Milled Flax Seed and Bob's Red Mill calls it Flax Seed Meal. When used in baking, Milled Flax Seed gives low carb baked goods a heartier, more wheat-like flavor. It is also a wonderful source of omega-3 fatty acids and fiber.

Sugar Substitutes

Sugar substitutes have been a great source of debate over the years. I would like to make it perfectly clear that the only reason I recommend Splenda is that it is what we have used to lose our weight and it is also what we use when testing our recipes. Unless otherwise noted, all sugar substitute used in this book is for "bulk" sugar substitute that measures cup for cup like regular sugar. This is usually found in boxes or large bags in the baking aisle. Sugar substitute in packets (for coffee, etc) is far more concentrated and does not measure the same as sugar... using these packets would result in recipes that are far too sweet!

You may use any sugar substitute you wish when preparing these recipes as long as they are suitable for cooking, as some substitutes lose their sweetness when baked. While we did not have the luxury when we first started on low carb, many entirely natural sugar substitutes are now available and can be used as you wish. We simply do not like to suggest anything that we didn't eat during our initial weight loss. We used Splenda.

Kosher Salt

I've never met a chef that cooks with table salt! We chefs use kosher salt, which has a much larger, fluffier grain than ordinary salt and usually doesn't contain any additives that may be found in other salts. Because of the fluffier grains, kosher salt takes up more volume and is actually more precise to measure. The difference between ¼ teaspoon and ½ teaspoon of table salt is actually quite staggering, sodium wise—but the difference between those measurements in kosher salt is about half—making it easier to get just the right level of salt in a recipe. Kosher salt is available near the ordinary salt in your grocery store and is usually sold in black or red boxes.

In a pinch, you can substitute table salt in place of the kosher salt, but must cut the amount used down by ½. Of course, if you are watching your sodium intake, all salt used in these recipes can be reduced or cut entirely according to your dietary needs.

NOTE: About Gluten

I have found that many of my recipes are popular with people that require gluten-free diets. Nearly all of the recipes in this book are gluten-free, and, to the best of my knowledge, all of them can be made gluten-free as long as you ensure that you purchase gluten-free brands of soy sauce, Worcestershire sauce, and other things that may contain trace amounts of hidden gluten.

PANTRY LIST

This is a list of the most commonly used ingredients in this book and a great indication of what you should keep in your house when living a low carb lifestyle.

Spice Cabinet

Baking powder

Basil

Bay leaves

Black pepper

Canola oil

Cayenne pepper

Chili powder

Cream of tartar

Cumin

Garlic powder

Ground cinnamon

Italian seasoning

Kosher salt

Nutmeg

Olive oil

Onion powder

Oregano

Paprika

Pumpkin pie spice

Thyme

Vanilla extract

Vegetable oil spray

White pepper

Pantry

Almond flour or raw almonds

Canned pumpkin

Dijon mustard

Garlic bulbs

Milled flax seed

Pecans

Red onions

Roasted red peppers

Soy flour

Spaghetti squash

Sugar substitute

Unsweetened baking chocolate

Unsweetened cocoa powder

Worcestershire sauce

Fridge

Butter

Cilantro

Cream Cheese

Eggs

Fresh herbs

Half and half

Heavy cream

Lemons

Parmesan cheese

Parsley

Red bell peppers

Ricotta cheese

BREAKFAST AND BRUNCH

Prep Time	Cook Time	Serves
15 min	55 min	8

Asparagus and Cheese Soufflé

Calories: 165 | Fat: 10.5g | Protein: 13g | Fiber: 2g | **Net Carbs: 4g**

Don't let the name "soufflé" scare you away from this amazing breakfast bake that's big enough to feed a crowd. With asparagus, yellow squash, roasted red peppers, and two types of cheese inside light and fluffy eggs, this is a gourmet dish that anyone can make and enjoy.

SHOPPING LIST

Vegetable oil spray

1 tablespoon vegetable oil

¼ cup diced red onion

1 medium yellow squash, cut into ¼-inch-thick half-moons

1 pound thin asparagus, bottoms trimmed and cut into 1-inch lengths

½ cup roasted red pepper strips

2 tablespoons thinly sliced scallions

6 large eggs

¼ cup heavy cream

½ teaspoon kosher salt

¼ teaspoon black pepper

Pinch of freshly ground nutmeg

1 cup shredded Swiss cheese

½ cup grated Parmesan cheese

Fresh herbs, for garnish

PREHEAT the oven to 400°F. Spray a 9x5 loaf pan with vegetable oil spray, line the bottom of the pan with a piece of parchment paper, and then spray the parchment paper with the oil spray.

HEAT the vegetable oil in a large skillet over medium-high heat. Add the onion, squash, and asparagus, and sauté 3 minutes.

REMOVE from the heat and stir in the red pepper strips and scallions. Drain well, transfer to a bowl, and let cool.

IN a mixing bowl, whisk together the eggs, cream, salt, pepper, and nutmeg. Stir in the cheeses and cooled vegetables.

POUR the mixture into the prepared pan and top with another piece of vegetable oil-sprayed parchment paper.

PLACE the loaf pan in a deep baking dish filled with 2 inches of tap water (to create a water bath) and place on the center oven rack.

BAKE until the center of the soufflé is firm and a toothpick inserted into it comes out clean, about 50 minutes.

REMOVE the soufflé from the oven and let cool for 10 minutes. Run a butter knife around the edges of the pan to release. Turn the soufflé out onto a cutting board and remove the parchment paper. Cut into 8 slices and serve hot, garnished with fresh herbs, if desired.

HELPFUL HINTS

While this is truly great when first prepared, it is also quite good served chilled as well. You can even slice it up into cubes and serve them as a chilled appetizer.

Raspberry Drop Scones

Calories: 125 | Fat: 9.5g | Protein: 5.5g | Fiber: 2.5g | **Net Carbs: 3g**

I can't believe I've never tried my hand at making low carb scones before; breakfast pastries always seemed out of reach until I broke down and found these to be ridiculously easy and delicious. Almond flour is just one magical ingredient I keep up my sleeve—conjuring up a nutty flavor and mystical texture that will surely transport you, as it did me, to that nice place you go when you begin your day with something sweet.

SHOPPING LIST

2 large eggs, beaten until frothy

1 cup almond flour

⅓ cup bulk sugar substitute (recommended: Splenda)

1 ½ teaspoons baking powder

1 ½ teaspoons vanilla extract

½ cup fresh raspberries

HELPFUL HINTS

If your batter is too thin to hold any form at all, simply add more almond flour until it is the consistency of a loose cookie dough.

1 PREHEAT the oven to 375°F and line a sheet pan with parchment paper.

2 IN a large bowl, combine all of the ingredients, except for the raspberries, and mix well to create a batter.

3 GENTLY fold the raspberries into the batter and use a tablespoon to drop 6 evenly spaced scones on the lined pan (about 2 heaping tablespoons for each scone).

4 BAKE for about 15 minutes until scones begin to lightly brown. Let cool for 10 minutes before removing from the parchment paper and serving warm.

BRUNCH

Blueberry Dream Stuffed Pancakes

Calories: 255 | Fat: 21g | Protein: 9.5g | Fiber: 4g | **Net Carbs: 6g**

Make these once and you will dream about them every day until you make them again! I say that you should row, row, row your boat into the kitchen to make these because life is but a Blueberry Dream—Stuffed Pancake!

SHOPPING LIST

4 ounces cream cheese, softened

½ cup fresh blueberries, may use frozen if well drained

Vegetable oil spray

2 large eggs

¼ cup water

1 tablespoon vanilla extract

½ cup almond flour

¼ cup milled flax seed

¼ cup bulk sugar substitute (recommended: Splenda)

1 teaspoon baking powder

HELPFUL HINTS

Without filling, the pancakes freeze perfectly; just put a small piece of parchment paper in between each cake and then microwave to serve anytime!

1 In a small bowl, mix the cream cheese and blueberries together with a fork until combined. Set aside.

2 Grease a griddle or large non-stick skillet with vegetable oil spray and heat over medium-high heat.

3 Mix all remaining ingredients in a bowl until well blended and the batter is a mud-like consistency. (Add a bit more water if too thick or a bit more almond flour if too thin).

4 Pour 8 thin cakes on the hot griddle and cook on the first side for 3 to 4 minutes until browned; then flip and cook for another minute or so to finish. Remove from heat.

5 Let pancakes cool for just a minute before filling by topping each with a tablespoon of the blueberry cream cheese mixture and loosely rolling up. Serve 2 per person, garnished with more blueberries and lemon zest, if desired.

Lemon Poppy Muffins

Calories: 125 | Fat: 10g | Protein: 5.5g | Fiber: 2g | **Net Carbs: 3g**

These muffins are a true classic that has been reinvented for the low carb lifestyle. Honestly, you never realize how much you like something like a Lemon Poppy Muffin until you have to reinvent it like we did!

BRUNCH

SHOPPING LIST

Vegetable oil spray

4 large eggs

⅓ cup lemon juice

¼ cup water

2 teaspoons lemon zest

2 teaspoons vanilla extract

2 cups almond flour

¾ cup bulk sugar substitute (recommended: Splenda)

1 tablespoon poppy seeds

2 teaspoons baking powder

HELPFUL HINTS

For a uniform and clean look, make the almond flour from blanched almonds without the brown skins.

1 PLACE oven rack in the center position and preheat to 375°F. Grease a 12-cup muffin pan with vegetable oil spray. (Use a silicone muffin pan for best results.)

2 IN a large bowl, beat eggs until frothy. Add the lemon juice, water, lemon zest, and vanilla extract, and beat to combine.

3 ADD all remaining ingredients and mix well to create a batter.

4 FILL each of the greased muffin cups ⅔ of the way full.

5 BAKE 20 to 25 minutes, until the tops of the muffins turn a light golden brown and a toothpick stuck into the center of one comes out mostly clean.

6 COOL on a wire rack. For best flavor, serve chilled.

Pistachio Pound Cake Minis

Calories: 250 | Fat: 23g | Protein: 7g | Fiber: 2g | **Net Carbs: 3g**

These little pound cakes have chopped pistachios baked right in. While we love the look of the little loaves, large muffin cups can be used in a pinch. Makes 8 loaves with 2 servings per loaf.

SHOPPING LIST

Vegetable oil spray

¾ cup butter, softened

6 large eggs, beaten until frothy

6 ounces cream cheese, softened

1 ½ teaspoons vanilla extract

1 ½ teaspoons lemon juice

2 ½ cups almond flour

1 ¼ cups bulk sugar substitute (recommended: Splenda)

2 teaspoons baking powder

½ cup chopped pistachios

HELPFUL HINTS

For a uniform and clean look, make the almond flour from blanched almonds without the brown skins.

1 PLACE oven rack in the center position and preheat to 325°F. Grease an 8 count mini loaf pan with vegetable oil spray. Cut 8 strips of parchment paper to line each of the 8 loaf compartments.

2 WITH an electric mixer on high speed, whip together the butter and cream cheese. Add the eggs, vanilla extract, and lemon juice, and blend until smooth, about 1 minute

3 ADD all remaining ingredients and mix by hand until all is combined and a batter is formed.

4 POUR an equal amount of the batter into each of the 8 mini loaf compartments.

5 BAKE 35 minutes, or until the tops are a light golden brown and a toothpick inserted into the center comes out mostly clean. Let cool at least 5 minutes before removing from the pan. Serve warm or chilled.

BRUNCH

Cinnamon Toast Pancakes

Calories: 160 | Fat: 11g | Protein: 7g | Fiber: 4g | **Net Carbs: 4g**

These pancakes are loaded with heart-healthy almonds and milled flax seed that is loaded with omega-3 fatty acids. While milled flax seed might not sound like the most delicious thing in the world, I think we can all get behind the great flavor of cinnamon toast! Drizzle with a small amount of light agave nectar for a low-glycemic take on syrup without the sugar alcohols found in sugar-free maple syrups.

SHOPPING LIST

Vegetable oil spray

BATTER

2 large eggs

¼ cup water

1 tablespoon vanilla extract

½ cup almond flour

¼ cup milled flax seed

¼ cup bulk sugar substitute (recommended: Splenda)

1 teaspoon baking powder

⅛ teaspoon salt

CINNAMON SPRINKLE

¼ teaspoon cinnamon

1 tablespoon bulk sugar substitute

Butter (may use light, trans-fat free buttery spread)

Fresh blueberries or strawberries, for garnish

1 GREASE a griddle or large skillet with vegetable oil spray and heat over medium-high heat.

2 MIX all the batter ingredients in a bowl with a wooden spoon until well blended.

3 POUR approximately 16 mini-cakes onto the hot griddle, and cook on the first side for 3 to 4 minutes until almost done, and then flip and cook for just another minute or so to finish. You may need to do this in 2 to 3 batches (as we use a very large electric griddle).

4 COMBINE the cinnamon and sugar substitute and sprinkle over the hot cakes before serving. If desired, top with a pat of melted butter or fat-free margarine and garnish with fresh berries.

HELPFUL HINTS

For a real treat, top with no sugar added whipped cream. While we often whip our own, most grocery stores now carry real "no sugar added" whipped heavy cream in a can (Land-O-Lakes brand).

Pecan Granola

Calories: 120 | Fat: 10g | Protein: 5g | Fiber: 4g | **Net Carbs: 1.5g**

Granola is just one of those things with a nutty crunch that's perfect in yogurt, on its own for a quick snack to munch on during the day, or even as a topping for whipped cream on dessert. You simply can't make enough, because before you know it, it's gone!

SHOPPING LIST

Vegetable oil spray

1 cup almond flour

1 cup milled flax seed

½ cup chopped pecans

1 cup bulk sugar substitute (recommended: Splenda)

½ teaspoon ground cinnamon

3 large egg whites, beaten until very frothy

HELPFUL HINTS

Lay a sheet of saran wrap over top the raw mixture in the lined sheet pan in step 3 for an easier, cleaner process; just remember to remove the plastic wrap before baking.

1 PREHEAT the oven to 300°F. Line a sheet pan with parchment paper and spray it with vegetable oil.

2 IN a large bowl, combine all of the ingredients, except the egg whites, and mix well.

3 FOLD in the frothy beaten egg whites until all is combined into a thick paste-like batter. Spread the batter evenly over the lined pan, pressing down with your hands to make a thin layer. Bake for about 25 to 30 minutes, depending on the thickness, or until granola feels a bit hard to the touch and can be pulled away from the pan at the edges.

4 LET cool for 20 minutes before removing from the parchment paper and breaking into large pieces. Keep stored in an airtight container on the counter.

BRUNCH

Prep Time	Cook Time	Serves
10 min	20 min	6

Strawberries and Mascarpone Cream Crêpes

Calories: 150 | Fat: 12g | Protein: 8g | Fiber: 0.5g | **Net Carbs: 2.5g**

Just as we have our pancakes, the French have their crêpes - only they stuff theirs and roll them up the way you would an open-ended burrito. Perfect for breakfast or dessert, these low carb beauties won't leave you feeling guilty!

SHOPPING LIST

½ cup whole milk ricotta cheese

4 large eggs

¼ cup bulk sugar substitute (recommended: Splenda)

1 ½ teaspoons cinnamon

½ teaspoon vanilla extract

½ cup chopped fresh strawberries

¼ cup mascarpone cheese

3 tablespoons butter

Sliced strawberries, for garnish

HELPFUL HINTS

You can cut each crêpe in half to create 12 servings out of the 6 crêpes. Using a 5 to 6-inch pan will yield around 8 to 10 crêpes.

1 ADD all of the ingredients, except the butter, berries, and mascarpone cheese, to a bowl and whisk well.

2 IN a separate bowl, mix the chopped strawberries and mascarpone together with a fork until the mixture starts to turn pink. Set aside.

3 MELT about ½ tablespoon of the butter in a 7 to 8-inch nonstick sauté pan over medium heat.

4 DROP ¼ cup of the crêpe mix in the hot pan and immediately tilt the pan back and forth to help spread the mixture thinly to the edges of the pan.

5 COOK for only about 1 minute until set, and carefully flip the crêpe, cooking for 1 additional minute. (I tilt the pan slightly and let the crêpe slide a bit over the edge of the pan before gently grabbing the crêpe by the edge with two fingertips and flipping instead of using a spatula that can break the fragile crêpe.) Repeat the last 2 steps until you've made 6 crêpes.

6 FILL each crêpe with 1 heaping tablespoon of the fresh strawberries and mascarpone mixture, and loosely roll up. Garnish with sliced strawberries.

Zucchini Muffins

Calories: 85 | Fat: 4.5g | Protein: 7g | Fiber: 1g | **Net Carbs: 4g**

These mostly savory muffins have just a touch of sweetness. Stuffing them with fresh diced zucchini adds not only extra nutrition but also color and moisture too! Serve them in place of dinner rolls, or try slicing them in half and using them in place of bread for sandwiches.

SHOPPING LIST

Vegetable oil spray

1 ½ cups soy flour

½ cup finely diced zucchini, with peel on

3 large eggs

¾ cup heavy cream

½ cup club soda

⅓ cup bulk sugar substitute (recommended: Splenda)

1 ½ teaspoons baking powder

HELPFUL HINTS

For best results, use silicone or nonstick muffin cups to prevent the muffins from sticking. You can also sprinkle the cups with sugar substitute to reduce sticking.

1 PREHEAT the oven to 375°F. Grease a 12-cup muffin pan with vegetable oil spray.

2 IN a large bowl, whisk the remaining ingredients until completely blended. Fill muffin cups about two-thirds full with the batter.

3 BAKE for 20 to 25 minutes, until the tops start to brown. (Be careful not to overcook or they will be very dry.) The muffins are done when lightly browned or when a toothpick inserted in the center of a muffin comes out clean.

4 REMOVE the muffins from the oven and let them cool for 5 minutes before removing from the pan. Serve warm with a pat of butter or at room temperature with cream cheese. Refrigerate any leftovers in a sealed container.

Apple Butter Pecan Bread

Calories: 155 | Fat: 12g | Protein: 6g | Fiber: 2.5g | **Net Carbs: 5g**

It wasn't until recently that Rachael realized how naturally low in carbs unsweetened applesauce is! Naturally, this opened up a whole new world of opportunities for her baking and this loaf of apple bread topped with buttery pecans is one fine example.

SHOPPING LIST

Vegetable oil spray

7 large eggs

1 ½ cups unsweetened applesauce

1 ½ teaspoons vanilla extract

2 ½ cups almond flour

1 ¼ cups bulk sugar substitute (recommended: Splenda)

2 teaspoons baking powder

1 ½ teaspoons ground cinnamon

⅓ cup chopped pecans

1 tablespoon butter, melted

HELPFUL HINTS

This is best served chilled, so we usually refrigerate for at least 2 hours before slicing.

1 PLACE oven rack in the center position and preheat to 325°F. Spray a 9x5-inch loaf pan with vegetable oil spray and then line with parchment paper.

2 IN a large bowl, beat eggs until frothy. Add the applesauce and vanilla extract, and beat to combine.

3 ADD almond flour, sugar substitute, baking powder, and cinnamon to the bowl, and mix well to create a batter.

4 POUR batter into the prepared loaf pan and spread out evenly.

5 COMBINE pecans and butter, and spread over top of the batter in the pan.

6 BAKE about 1 hour, until the top turns a light golden brown and a toothpick inserted into the center comes out mostly clean.

7 COOL on a wire rack before slicing into 8 thick slices and then slicing those in half again for 16 servings.

Baked Bacon-Wrapped Cheesy Eggs

Calories: 125 | Fat: 9g | Protein: 9.5g | Fiber: 0g | **Net Carbs: 1g**

Breakfast can be one of those meals you'd rather skip on occasion due to the effort it takes, but these eggs, wrapped in bacon, topped with cheese, and then baked in a muffin pan, offer a simple solution. We make it all the time, but we are very selective about our American cheese choice since many cheese foods contain a lot of additives.

BRUNCH

SHOPPING LIST

Vegetable oil spray

6 strips cooked bacon

6 large eggs

3 slices American cheese, cut in half to make 6 pieces

HELPFUL HINTS

Serve these bacon-wrapped eggs with a steak knife for cutting through the bacon. To make these even easier, the pre-cooked bacon you can buy at the store works perfect in this recipe!

1 PLACE oven rack in the center position and preheat the to 375°F.

2 SPRAY a 6-cup muffin pan with vegetable oil and line each cup with a strip of cooked bacon so it circles the inside.

3 CRACK an egg into each of the cups, trying to keep the yolks unbroken, and bake for about 12 minutes, or until the egg whites are cooked.

4 REMOVE the pan from the oven and top each cooked egg with a half slice of American cheese.

5 PLACE back in the oven for 1 or 2 minutes more, just until the cheese begins to melt.

6 REMOVE and let stand for another minute before taking each bacon-wrapped egg out of the pan using a fork or small rubber spatula. Serve hot, garnished with fresh parsley, if desired.

White Pizza Frittata

Calories: 260 | Fat: 19g | Protein: 19g | Fiber: 0g | **Net Carbs: 3g**

Frittatas are Italy's equivalent to the French omelet. Served open-faced instead of folded, they are sliced to share instead of keeping them all to yourself. Sharing is better in my opinion, as this version reminds me of a white pizza that is too good to keep all to yourself!

BRUNCH

SHOPPING LIST

2 tablespoons butter

CHEESE TOPPING

8 ounces whole-milk ricotta cheese

8 ounces shredded mozzarella cheese

¼ cup grated Parmesan cheese

1 teaspoon Italian seasoning

½ teaspoon garlic powder

⅛ teaspoon black pepper

EGG MIXTURE

10 large eggs

¼ cup heavy cream

¼ cup hot water

½ teaspoon salt

¼ teaspoon grated nutmeg

HELPFUL HINTS

For added pizza flavor that will have your whole house smelling like a pizza parlor, simply sprinkle ⅛ teaspoon of dry oregano and drizzle a couple drops of olive oil over the top of the frittata just before baking!

1 PREHEAT the oven to 325°F.

2 IN a large bowl, combine the cheese topping ingredients together and mix well.

3 PLACE all of the egg mixture ingredients together in a separate bowl and whisk well.

4 MELT the butter in a large oven-proof skillet over medium to high heat.

5 POUR the egg mixture into the pan, and using a rubber spatula, slowly push the cooked egg from one side of the pan to the other to allow all of the raw egg to reach the bottom of the pan and to prevent the bottom from burning.

6 ONCE the frittata is cooked on the bottom with the top still a bit runny, spoon the cheese topping evenly on top.

7 COVER the pan with aluminum foil and bake for 12 to 15 minutes (remove the foil for the last few minutes of baking to brown the cheese).

8 CUT into 8 portions and serve hot as you would pizza.

Prep Time	Cook Time	Serves
10 min	15 min	6

Sausage and Egg Not-Muffins

Calories: 235 | Fat: 18g | Protein: 16g | Fiber: 0g | **Net Carbs: 0.5g**

I love cooking eggs in muffin pans, as you can make them not only cook uniformly and look perfect, but you can also prepare breakfast for a crowd without overcrowding a skillet! While these are closer to miniature quiches, they remind me of sausage and egg breakfast sandwiches.

SHOPPING LIST

Vegetable oil spray

6 ounces cooked breakfast sausage, crumbled or chopped

6 large eggs

⅛ teaspoon salt

⅛ teaspoon black pepper

1 cup shredded Cheddar cheese

HELPFUL HINTS

This is also extremely good when you top each with a thin slice of cream cheese instead of the Cheddar. Or try topping with a dollop of herbed cream cheese spread!

1 PLACE the oven rack in the center position and preheat the to 375°F. Spray a 6-cup muffin pan with vegetable oil spray.

2 ADD equal amounts of cooked sausage to each of the muffin cups.

3 WHISK the eggs together with the salt and pepper, and pour equally into each of the 6 sausage-lined muffin cups.

4 TOP each cup with an equal amount of the Cheddar cheese and bake for 12 to 15 minutes, just until the eggs are slightly firm and cheese is bubbly

5 REMOVE from the oven and let cool for 2 minutes before taking each Sausage and Egg Not-Muffin out of the pan using a fork or small rubber spatula. Serve hot, garnished with fresh chopped chives or parsley, if desired.

V.G 2/28/14
DOUBLE

Cheese Danish Dreams

Calories: 260 | Fat: 24g | Protein: 10.5g | Fiber: 0g | **Net Carbs: 2g**

Do you have 2 minutes? If you do, that's all it takes to avoid having dreams of sugary cheese Danishes dancing in your head, because you can be eating these decadent and satisfying no-sugar-added cheese Danish dreams instead! So the next time you need to curb a sugar attack, try this anytime cravings-buster!

BRUNCH

SHOPPING LIST

4 ounces cream cheese, softened

2 large eggs

2 tablespoons bulk sugar substitute (recommended: Splenda)

1 teaspoon vanilla extract

⅛ teaspoon ground cinnamon

HELPFUL HINTS

I like to top with additional cinnamon and sugar substitute before serving. Or add fresh berries or sliced almonds to the center for something even better!

1 ADD all of the ingredients to a bowl and mix with a fork until smooth.

2 POUR the mixture evenly into the bottom of 2 microwaveable cereal bowls and microwave on high for 2 minutes, rotating the bowls every 30 seconds until springy around the outside and soft in the center.

3 USE a spatula to remove Danishes from bowls, and let cool 2 to 3 minutes before serving.

MUFFIN PAN (6)
HIGH 3 - 3.5 MIN

LUNCHTIME FAVORITES

Prep Time	Chill Time	Serves
20 min	60 min	8

Old-Fashioned Egg Mock Potato Salad

Calories: 180 | Fat: 13g | Protein: 6g | Fiber: 2g | **Net Carbs: 3g**

There's egg salad, there's potato salad, and then there's this recipe - a reinvention of a dish my mother used to make that my family has enjoyed since forever! Cauliflower sits neutrally on the tongue, just like potatoes do, but absorbs other flavors the way a good steak does. I'm sure you'll agree (after tasting, of course), that it's simply old-fashioned goodness, reinvented, at its best!

SHOPPING LIST

1 large head cauliflower, cleaned

6 hard-boiled large eggs, chopped

2 stalks celery, finely diced

1 cup mayonnaise

½ teaspoon yellow table mustard

½ teaspoon kosher salt

¼ teaspoon black pepper

⅛ teaspoon garlic powder

Paprika, for garnish

Fresh parsley, chopped, for garnish

CHOP the cauliflower into small pieces (should make about 4 cups).

SET a large pot of water over high heat and bring to a boil.

COOK the cauliflower pieces in the boiling water for about 5 minutes, until tender.

DRAIN cauliflower and immerse in an ice water bath to stop the cooking process.

DRAIN cauliflower well and then pat dry between several layers of paper towels.

PLACE the cauliflower in a bowl with all of the remaining ingredients, except the garnishes, and fold together.

SPRINKLE with the paprika and parsley, and chill for at least 1 hour before serving.

HELPFUL HINTS

Be sure to fold all of the ingredients together until the salad is a nice yellow color.

Curry Chicken Lettuce Wraps

Calories: 170 | Fat: 9.5g | Protein: 18.5g | Fiber: 1g | **Net Carbs: 2g**

It has always seemed to me that wraps were a convenient way to enjoy things. This particular recipe calls for a natural, zero-calorie alternative to the typical wrap packaging—lettuce! Now throw in some protein-packed chicken, snow peas, walnuts, and curry to spice things up and you've got a low carb wrap that's truly one-of-a-kind.

LUNCH

SHOPPING LIST

2 tablespoons canola oil

1 pound chicken breast, sliced

½ cup julienned red onion

½ cup chicken stock

½ cup sliced snow peas

⅓ cup chopped walnuts

1 tablespoon curry powder

1 teaspoon bulk sugar substitute (recommended: Splenda)

½ teaspoon kosher salt

¼ teaspoon black pepper

¼ teaspoon garlic powder

6 large iceberg lettuce leaves

1 HEAT the oil in a large skillet over medium-high heat.

2 ADD the chicken and onions, and cook for about 5 minutes until the sliced chicken is cooked throughout.

3 STIR in the remaining ingredients, except the lettuce, and cook for 2 to 3 additional minutes, or until any liquid reduces and the vegetables are tender. Remove from heat.

4 DIVIDE the mixture between 6 or more lettuce leaves, roll up, and secure with a toothpick to serve. Garnish with fresh cantaloupe slices or unsweetened coconut flakes.

HELPFUL HINTS

This simple Curry recipe works great with steak, pork, or even seafood, so utilize previously cooked leftover meats and you'll never look at leftovers the same way again!

Caribbean Sweet Potato Salad

Calories: 200 | Fat: 15g | Protein: 2g | Fiber: 2g | **Net Carbs: 13g**

Working as a chef in south Florida while growing up, there was always a Caribbean influence in the kitchen. From Cuba to Puerto Rico and the Dominicans to Haiti, so many cultures were represented through traditions such as the use of peppers, tropical fruits, herbs, and fragrant island spices. This recipe has all that and then some and tastes like a German potato salad gone tropical.

LUNCH

SHOPPING LIST

3 medium sweet potatoes, cut into ½ inch cubes (4 cups)

2 tablespoons Dijon mustard

¼ cup fresh lime juice

2 tablespoons honey, may use sugar substitute

¼ teaspoon salt

⅛ teaspoon black pepper

1 teaspoon chopped fresh cilantro leaves, may use dry

2 tablespoons chopped red onion

1 small clove garlic, minced

½ cup olive oil

¼ cup diced green bell pepper

¼ cup shelled roasted peanuts

1 Cook the cubed sweet potatoes in boiling water for about 6 to 8 minutes, until tender.

2 Drain and cool potatoes under cold running water. Strain well and reserve.

3 Add all remaining ingredients, except the diced bell pepper and peanuts, to a bowl and whisk vigorously until fully combined and slightly thickened.

4 Fold the diced bell pepper, peanuts, and cooked sweet potatoes into the dressing.

5 Cover and refrigerate for 2 hours before serving garnished with fresh cilantro and lime wedges, if desired.

HELPFUL HINTS

Use a food processor or blender to make quick work of the dressing, and add a bit of mayonnaise or sour cream to make this salad supreme!

Sweet Potato Slaw

Calories: 155 | Fat: 9g | Protein: 2.5g | Fiber: 2.5g | **Net Carbs: 14g**

Lately, there seems to always be sweet potatoes in the house—I mean, all the time! I guess it's because we know they are healthy and we've been eating them regularly now for a few years—and without putting on weight! That's the true litmus test around here as to whether a food is not only good for you but good for the low carb lifestyle—and the proof is in the pudding—or sweet potato slaw as it is here!

SHOPPING LIST

½ cup mayonnaise, may use plain yogurt

⅓ cup sour cream

¼ cup bulk sugar substitute (recommended: Splenda)

½ cup chopped walnuts, may use pecans

1 tablespoon balsamic vinegar

2 cups shredded sweet potatoes, blanched 30 seconds in boiling water, cooled, and drained well

2 red apples, shredded

¼ teaspoon salt

⅛ teaspoon black pepper

¼ teaspoon ground cinnamon

⅛ teaspoon ground ginger

1 MIX all ingredients together in a large bowl, tossing to combine.

2 CHILL for 2 hours before serving garnished with walnut halves, if desired.

HELPFUL HINTS

It's easy to shred the sweet potato using the larger holes of a cheese grater, but it's even easier if you have a food processor with a cheese shredder attachment blade!

Pecan and Pear Coleslaw

Calories: 130 | Fat: 9g | Protein: 1.5g | Fiber: 3g | **Net Carbs: 9g**

A coleslaw recipe this good comes along about once every decade. I know this because it was 10 years ago that Rachel made her famous Waldorf Coleslaw (see page: 49). With pecans and pears, I think she's topped her classic, but I say there's room enough for both!

SHOPPING LIST

½ cup mayonnaise

⅓ cup sour cream

¼ cup bulk sugar substitute (recommended: Splenda)

½ cup chopped pecans (may use sliced or slivered almonds)

2 tablespoons red wine vinegar

12 ounces shredded green cabbage

4 ounces shredded red cabbage

2 ripe pears, cut into small cubes

½ teaspoon salt

⅛ teaspoon black pepper

¼ teaspoon ground nutmeg

⅛ teaspoon ground ginger

1 Mix all ingredients together in a large bowl, tossing to combine.

2 For best flavor, chill 2 hours before serving garnished with pecan halves, if desired.

HELPFUL HINTS

To make this salad even lower in carbs, simply replace the pears with 1 cup of sliced strawberries.

You can easily substitute a 16-ounce bag of shredded coleslaw mix for the two types of cabbage used in this recipe.

Green and Yellow Bean Salad

Calories: 100 | Fat: 7.5g | Protein: 2.5g | Fiber: 2.5g | **Net Carbs: 4g**

This simple, chilled green bean salad is a great hit at picnics or parties. Adding yellow wax beans and chopped walnuts makes this seem more elegant than the effort needed to prepare it.

SHOPPING LIST

½ pound green beans

½ pound yellow wax beans

3 tablespoons olive oil

2 tablespoons red wine vinegar

1 tablespoon Dijon mustard

1 teaspoon honey

¾ teaspoon Italian seasoning

¼ teaspoon salt

⅛ teaspoon pepper

3 tablespoons finely diced red onion

1 cup grape tomatoes, halved

¼ cup chopped walnuts

HELPFUL HINTS

If yellow wax beans are too difficult to find, simply doubling the amount of regular green beans in this recipe will suffice.

LUNCH

1 SNAP hard ends from green and wax beans, and discard. Place in boiling water and boil for 4 to 5 minutes, or until crisp-tender. Drain and rinse under cool water.

2 IN a large bowl, whisk olive oil, red wine vinegar, Dijon mustard, honey, Italian seasoning, salt, and pepper until fully combined.

3 ADD red onion, grape tomatoes, chopped walnuts, and the cooked green beans to the bowl and toss until all are coated.

4 COVER and refrigerate for at least 1 hour before serving.

Grilled Caesar Salad

Calories: 55 | Fat: 5g | Protein: 1g | Fiber: 0.5g | **Net Carbs: 1.5g**

Romaine hearts are an easy-to-prepare and inexpensive lettuce you can often find in packs of three. Fine dining restaurants downtown charge a fortune for a warm salad like this one, so why not make it at home when it only takes 5 minutes!

SHOPPING LIST

3 romaine lettuce hearts, cut in half lengthwise to make 6 pieces

2 tablespoons olive oil

Kosher salt and black pepper

2 tablespoons fresh lemon juice

1 tablespoon lemon zest

2 cloves fresh garlic, thinly sliced or chopped

2 tablespoons shaved Parmesan cheese

HELPFUL HINTS

While I am grilling the romaine, I like to throw veggies such as cherry tomatoes, red onion, and even mushrooms alongside it, topping my grilled salad like I would a pizza!

1 LIGHT or preheat a grill to medium-high to high.

2 LAY the romaine lettuce heart halves face up on a sheet pan, drizzle all with olive oil, and sprinkle liberally with salt and pepper.

3 GRILL the romaine hearts face down for about 3 minutes, or just until grill marks form; turn over and cook for about 2 minutes more.

4 REMOVE from heat, drizzle with lemon juice, and serve immediately topped with lemon zest, fresh garlic, and Parmesan cheese.

LUNCH

Prep Time	Cook Time	Serves
10 min	8 min	6

Grilled Zucchini and Pecan Salad

Calories: 85 | Fat: 7g | Protein: 2.5g | Fiber: 2g | **Net Carbs: 3.5g**

Zucchini has to be one my favorite summertime vegetables and there's no shortage of ways you can use them! They've definitely earned my respect over the years and never seem to fail as one of those low-in-carbs ingredients I just love to throw on the grill.

SHOPPING LIST

4 medium whole zucchini, cut in half lengthwise to make 8 pieces

2 tablespoons olive oil

Kosher salt and black pepper

2 tablespoons fresh lemon juice

1 clove fresh garlic, minced

1 tablespoon chopped fresh basil leaves, may use parsley

2 tablespoons chopped pecans

2 tablespoons shaved Parmesan cheese

HELPFUL HINTS

Yellow squash works great in place of the zucchini, or try using both! Also, try adding some cooked bacon pieces with the pecans for some good 'ole down south decadence!

1 LIGHT or preheat a grill to medium-high to high.

2 LAY the zucchini halves face up on a sheet pan, drizzle all with olive oil, and sprinkle generously with salt and pepper.

3 GRILL the zucchini halves face down for about 4 minutes, or just until grill marks form; turn over and cook for about 4 minutes more.

4 REMOVE from heat and slice zucchini halves into ½ inch pieces. Add to a bowl with the lemon juice, minced garlic, chopped basil, and pecans.

5 TOSS well and serve warm or cold in 6 small dishes topped with Parmesan cheese and garnished with lemon zest and diced red peppers, if desired.

Waldorf Coleslaw

Calories: 105 | Fat: 8.5g | Protein: 2.5g | Fiber: 2g | **Net Carbs: 4g**

Waldorf salad has always been a favorite in our family, so it was only natural that Rachel would come up with this marriage of a Waldorf salad and coleslaw. While we've been making this recipe since my show on the Food Network, a few things have changed over the years—most notably the addition of thinly sliced celery—a Waldorf must!

SHOPPING LIST

½ cup sour cream

⅓ cup mayonnaise

⅓ cup bulk sugar substitute (or more to taste)

½ cup coarsely chopped walnuts

2 tablespoons red wine vinegar

12 ounces shredded green cabbage

4 ounces shredded red cabbage

3 stalks celery, thinly sliced

1 teaspoon kosher salt

⅛ teaspoon black pepper

¼ teaspoon ground nutmeg

1 MIX all ingredients together in a large bowl, tossing to combine.

2 FOR best flavor, chill 2 hours before serving.

HELPFUL HINTS

You can easily substitute a 16-ounce bag of shredded coleslaw mix for the two types of cabbage used in this recipe.

Radicchio Salad with Raspberry Vinaigrette

Calories: 165 | Fat: 12g | Protein: 4g | Fiber: 5.5g | **Net Carbs: 6g**

This upscale salad is secretly made with only a few simple ingredients. Rather than create the vinaigrette from scratch, we get all the fresh raspberry flavor by blending fresh raspberries into Italian dressing.

SHOPPING LIST

16 ounces Italian salad dressing (check that no sugar is added in the ingredients)

1 cup fresh raspberries

¼ cup bulk sugar substitute (recommended: Splenda)

1 head radicchio lettuce, leaves separated, rinsed, and dried

One 8-ounce bag fancy lettuce mix

2 Roma tomatoes, each cut into 4 wedges

8 ounces whole hearts of palm, cut into sticks

2 tablespoons finely diced red bell pepper

2 tablespoons finely diced green bell pepper

1 IN a blender or food processor, combine the Italian dressing, ½ cup of the raspberries, and the sugar substitute. Blend until smooth.

2 LINE a bowl or plate with whole radicchio leaves, and then pile the fancy lettuce mix high in the center. Place the tomato wedges around the plate in a starburst fashion and add the heart of palm sticks between the wedges.

3 SPRINKLE with the minced bell peppers.

4 POUR raspberry vinaigrette over the salad, top with the remaining ½ cup fresh raspberries, and serve. Store the remainder of the vinaigrette (for up to 2 weeks) in the refrigerator.

LUNCH

HELPFUL HINTS

Be sure to choose a regular Italian dressing when preparing this, as one with Parmesan cheese in it just doesn't go with the berries! Or make your own by mixing 4 parts oil to 1 part balsamic vinegar and adding 2 teaspoons Italian seasoning.

Easy Philly Steak Salad

Calories: 580 | Fat: 24g | Protein: 77g | Fiber: 2.5g | **Net Carbs: 4g**

Leftover steak can offer a variety of options when it comes to a mid-day meal, but the first that comes to mind is Philly-style steak! There's just something about the bell peppers that makes it so darn special! This crisp, yet warm salad, topped with your Philly favorites, including melted mozzarella cheese, is so satisfying and simple to make that you'll wonder why all that good stuff would ever need to be piled onto dense, carb-filled bread!

SHOPPING LIST

1 tablespoon butter or vegetable oil

1 cup sliced red and green bell peppers

12 ounces leftover cooked steak, shredded

¼ teaspoon garlic powder

Salt and pepper

1 cup shredded mozzarella cheese

10 ounces salad mix

1 HEAT the butter or oil in a large skillet over medium-high heat. Add the peppers, steak, and seasonings, and cook for about 5 minutes until the peppers are tender.

2 TURN the heat off. Top the hot steak and peppers with the cheese and let melt.

3 DIVIDE the salad greens evenly between 2 bowls.

4 DIVIDE the hot mixture evenly between the bowls of salad and serve immediately.

HELPFUL HINTS

You can also use frozen "minute" steaks to top this salad. Simply sauté or griddle according to the package directions.

If You Had Wings Too

Calories: 395 | Fat: 32g | Protein: 26g | Fiber: 0g | **Net Carbs: 0g**

When I originally wrote a recipe for simple fried chicken wings (without the carb-filled breading), I used my famous Blackening Spice to season them up, but in the last few years we've been making them in our house with my new Canadian Steak Seasoning instead. I like them so much better this way and can't imagine ever going back!

SHOPPING LIST

3 to 6 cups vegetable oil (more or less, depending on the pot used)

2 pounds fresh chicken wings, wing tips removed and discarded

Canadian Steak Seasoning (see page: 85)

HELPFUL HINTS

Lightly sprinkle the wings with additional Canadian Steak Seasoning right after removing from the hot oil for even more flavor.

1 PLACE a deep, heavy pot over medium-high heat and fill with at least 2 inches oil. Heat the oil to 375°F. (Portable deep fryers are great for this, but if you don't have one, you can use a candy thermometer—just be careful!)

2 COAT the chicken wings liberally with the Canadian Steak Seasoning, rubbing it in well with your hands.

3 CAREFULLY drop the seasoned wings into the hot oil—use a slotted spoon and wear mitts—and fry until golden crispy brown, 8 to 10 minutes. Remove and drain the wings on paper towels before serving.

Knife and Fork Chili Turkey Burgers

Calories: 220 | Fat: 12.5g | Protein: 26g | Fiber: 0g | **Net Carbs: 1.5g**

When eating low carb, it is a must to keep things outrageously unique, which is exactly what my wife Rachel kept in mind when she helped me come up with these bun-less beauties. Turkey is especially lean, so the diced onions and bell peppers add a much needed amount of moisture to the meat. Makes 10 burgers.

LUNCH

SHOPPING LIST

Vegetable oil spray

2 ½ pounds fresh ground turkey

1 cup shredded sharp Cheddar cheese

1 large egg

½ cup finely diced red bell pepper

¼ cup finely diced red onion

1 tablespoon no-sugar-added ketchup

1 tablespoon chili powder

1 teaspoon salt

¼ teaspoon black pepper

Pinch of cayenne pepper

Your favorite burger fixings

1 SPRAY a large sauté pan with vegetable oil and set aside.

2 PLACE all of the ingredients, except the extra fixings, into a bowl and mix well with your hands. (You may want to wear plastic gloves, since the chili powder may turn your hands red.)

3 FORM the meat mixture into 10 patties.

4 COOK the turkey burgers in the sauté pan over medium-high heat for 6 to 7 minutes on each side, until completely cooked throughout. (Poultry MUST be fully cooked. No medium-rare for these patties!)

5 SERVE as a meal with the traditional burger toppings or use your own low carb favorites!

HELPFUL HINTS

These can also be grilled; just make sure that the grill is preheated well and that you do not try to flip the burgers until they are well-marked or they stick to the grates.

Dinah's Pizza-Stuffed Eggplants

Calories: 610 | Fat: 41g | Protein: 40g | Fiber: 8g | **Net Carbs: 8g**

Dinah Moore started off as one of the most active members of my online community but quickly became a friend of our entire family due to her infectious personality and recipes like this one! Though this was one of her first attempts at cooking with eggplant, the results are so delicious that including her recipe in this book was a no-brainer!

SHOPPING LIST

2 medium eggplants

1 pound Italian sausage, casings removed

½ cup diced red onion

2 cloves garlic, minced

1 green bell pepper, diced

1 cup sliced button mushrooms

1 (15-ounce) can tomato sauce

½ cup black olives, chopped

1 tablespoon Italian seasoning

2 cups mozzarella cheese

HELPFUL HINTS

These can also be made with lean turkey Italian sausage and ½ of the Mozzarella cheese to cut the fat in this recipe by more than half.

1 PREHEAT the oven to 350°F. Cut the ends off of the eggplants and then slice in half lengthwise. Scoop all but ½-inch of the eggplant meat from the eggplant halves, leaving empty shells, and then dice and reserve the scooped eggplant. Place the empty eggplant shells in a 13x9 baking dish.

2 PLACE the Italian sausage, onion, and garlic in a large skillet over medium-high heat and cook, crumbling the sausage, until browned.

3 ADD the reserved eggplant flesh, bell pepper and mushrooms to the skillet and sauté an additional 3 minutes before draining well.

4 STIR in tomato sauce, olives, and Italian seasoning, and bring up to a simmer. Let simmer 5 minutes.

5 SPRINKLE ½ of the mozzarella cheese evenly over the inside of the eggplant shells and then top with an equal amount of the cooked sausage mixture.

6 TOP the stuffed eggplants with the remaining mozzarella cheese and bake 30 to 35 minutes. Let cool 5 minutes before serving.

APPETIZERS AND SNACKS

Pepperoni Chips and Easy Cheese Crackers

Calories: 150 | Fat: 13g | Protein: 6g | Fiber: 0g | **Net Carbs: 0g**

It's no secret that cheese and pepperoni are star-crossed lovers (in your mouth, anyway)! The real shocker here is that these crackers require little to no preparation before popping into the oven, making for one of the easiest ways to cure any oncoming snack attack!

SHOPPING LIST

PEPPERONI CHIPS

6 ounces thin-sliced pepperoni

CHEESE CRACKERS

2 slices deluxe American cheese (not "processed cheese food")

½ teaspoon salt

⅛ teaspoon chili powder

⅛ teaspoon garlic powder

HELPFUL HINTS

If you have a convection oven, be sure to turn the convection fan off before you bake or the pepperoni chips will fly right off the sheet pan!

PEPPERONI CHIPS

PREHEAT the oven to 425°F. Lay the pepperoni slices in a single layer on a baking sheet and bake for 8 to 10 minutes.

REMOVE the pan from the oven and soak up the excess grease by pressing paper towels against the pepperoni chips. Return the pan to the oven and bake an additional 2 to 4 minutes, until the pepperoni slices are very crispy.

EASY CHEESE CRACKERS

PREHEAT the oven to 400°F. Line a baking sheet with parchment paper.

STACK the slices of American cheese and cut them into 16 very small squares.

SEPARATE the cheese squares and transfer them to a small bowl. Add the salt, chili powder, and garlic powder, and toss to combine.

ARRANGE the 32 cheese pieces in 4 rows of 8 on the parchment paper-lined baking sheet, leaving as much space in between each as possible. (A silicone baking mat works perfectly here and you can use it over and over.)

BAKE until they puff up, are well browned (almost burnt), and crispy, about 7 to 8 minutes. If undercooked, they'll be soggy, so don't be afraid to check them and put them back in for more time, if needed.

COOL the crackers completely before serving since they will crisp up as they cool. Store on the counter in an airtight container for as long as a few days. Enjoy!

Open-Faced Jalapeño Poppers

Calories: 165 | Fat: 13g | Protein: 7.5g | Fiber: 0.5g | **Net Carbs: 1.5g**

Forget those frozen, breaded things you pop into your mouth one by one! These easy, cheese-stuffed appetizers will have you loving fresh jalapeños - even if you don't usually care for spicy foods. They're even addictive as leftovers right out of the refrigerator.

SHOPPING LIST

Vegetable oil spray

2 cups shredded Colby-jack or Mexican blend cheese

8 ounces cream cheese, softened

¼ cup cooked bacon crumbles

½ teaspoon chili powder

¼ teaspoon kosher salt

¼ teaspoon garlic powder

12 large fresh jalapeño peppers (about 1 pound), cut in half lengthwise and seeded.

1 teaspoon sliced fresh scallions or chives, for garnish

1 PREHEAT the oven to 300°F and spray a sheet pan with vegetable oil.

2 ADD all the ingredients, except the peppers and chives, to a bowl and mix well to combine.

3 WORKING over a sheet pan, spoon the cheese mixture into each of the 24 seeded jalapeño halves, overfilling them slightly.

4 BAKE for about 30 minutes before serving hot, topped with sliced scallions or chives, if desired.

HELPFUL HINTS

You can lessen the heat of fresh jalapeños by pre-baking the seeded halves on the sheet pan by themselves for about 10 minutes before stuffing and baking again. Or try using pickled jalapeños for an even milder version!

APPS

Cheesy Spinach Muffin Bites

Calories: 140 | Fat: 12.5g | Protein: 5g | Fiber: 1.5g | **Net Carbs: 2g**

These savory delights are a great start to any meal and a great addition to any party buffet. Parmesan and spinach make the perfect stuffing for just about anything—so why not muffins? Makes 24 mini muffin bites.

SHOPPING LIST

Vegetable oil spray

1 ½ cups almond flour

3 large eggs

¾ cup heavy cream, may use half and half

¼ cup Parmesan cheese

½ cup chopped frozen spinach, thawed and squeezed dry

2 tablespoons olive oil

1 tablespoon baking powder

¼ teaspoon salt

⅛ teaspoon garlic powder

HELPFUL HINTS

Add ¼ cup of finely diced ham or cooked bacon for an even more savory muffin.

1 PLACE oven rack in the center position and preheat to 350°F. Spray a 24-cup mini muffin pan with vegetable oil spray.

2 ADD all of the ingredients to a large bowl and whisk together until completely blended. The batter should be a mud-like consistency, so add a little water if too thick.

3 FILL each muffin cup about ⅔ of the way full with the batter.

4 BAKE 17 to 20 minutes, until muffins are lightly browned and a toothpick inserted into the center of a muffin comes out mostly clean.

5 REMOVE the muffins from the oven and let cool for 5 minutes before removing from the pan. Serve warm with a pat of butter or cream cheese, if desired. Keep refrigerated for up to 1 week

Tomato Basil Cheese Dip

Calories: 90 | Fat: 7.5g | Protein: 4g | Fiber: 0g | **Net Carbs: 1g**

Fresh basil leaves and ripe tomatoes are two things we never seem to run out of, thanks to Rachel's garden! And since we also keep a good amount of cream cheese on hand, we're always experimenting, which is how this recipe was born!

SHOPPING LIST

8 ounces cream cheese, softened

1 cup grated Parmesan cheese

½ cup diced tomatoes

1 tablespoon chopped fresh basil leaves

1 tablespoon lime juice (may use lemon)

¼ teaspoon kosher salt

¼ teaspoon garlic powder

⅛ teaspoon white pepper

1 ADD all of the ingredients to a bowl and mix well.

2 CHILL at least 1 hour before serving as a dip for vegetable crudités, pork rinds, or even cheese crisps!

APPS

HELPFUL HINTS

Try cutting the top off a bell pepper, seeding it, and using it as a bowl to serve this dip in.

Prosciutto Wrapped Asparagus

Calories: 80 | Fat: 5g | Protein: 7g | Fiber: 1g | **Net Carbs: 1.5g**

These simple appetizers are a really great way to make two notoriously luxurious ingredients go a long way. While prosciutto and asparagus are often thought of as expensive, if you catch the asparagus on sale, you can prepare more than two dozen of these for around $7.

SHOPPING LIST

1 pound fresh asparagus, bottoms trimmed

2 tablespoons extra virgin olive oil

¼ teaspoon kosher salt

⅛ teaspoon black pepper

½ pound thinly sliced prosciutto

1 teaspoon lemon zest, optional as garnish

HELPFUL HINTS

Prepare these in advance and refrigerate for a quick and easy appetizer that you can pull out just as your guests arrive.

1 PREHEAT the oven to 450°F.

2 TOSS asparagus in olive oil, salt, and pepper and place on a heavy sheet pan.

3 BAKE 8 to 10 minutes, just until tender. Remove and let cool completely.

4 WRAP each asparagus spear in a thin slice of prosciutto, leaving both ends showing. Serve slightly chilled, sprinkled with lemon zest if desired.

APPS

Green Goddess Dip

Calories: 80 | Fat: 7g | Protein: 1g | Fiber: 0g | **Net Carbs: 3g**

I still remember when Green Goddess was just about the most popular salad dressing (and dip) around. At some point, though, Ranch just swooped down and all but knocked Green Goddess out of everyone's consciousness! It's a real shame because I really love the fresh, herby tarragon and hint of anchovy (the most important ingredient in Caesar dressing) that sets Green Goddess apart from today's Ranch dressings and dips.

SHOPPING LIST

1 cup mayonnaise

¾ cup sour cream

1 tablespoon cider vinegar, may use lemon juice

3 tablespoons chopped fresh parsley

2 tablespoons chopped fresh tarragon leaves

½ teaspoon minced fresh garlic

2 canned anchovy fillets or 1 teaspoon anchovy paste

¼ teaspoon kosher salt

⅛ teaspoon black pepper

1 ADD all of the ingredients, except the chives, to a blender or food processor and pulse until well combined.

2 CHILL for at least 1 hour before serving as a dip for vegetable crudité.

APPS

HELPFUL HINTS

This also makes an amazing dip for my Open-Faced Jalapeño Poppers (see page: 63), Cheesy Cauliflower Fritters (see page: 83), or If You Had Wings Too chicken wings (see page: 53).

Roasted Pizza Peanuts

Calories: 305 | Fat: 27g | Protein: 13g | Fiber: 3.5g | **Net Carbs: 6g**

Roasting peanuts at home makes for an inexpensive, healthy snack. The aromas will also have you thinking you just walked into a baseball stadium and the game is about to begin! Batter up!

SHOPPING LIST

1 large bag raw peanuts in shell, 24 to 32 ounces

¼ cup olive oil

⅓ cup grated Parmesan cheese

½ teaspoon black pepper

½ teaspoon garlic powder

2 teaspoons kosher salt

HELPFUL HINTS

When the peanuts are hot out of the oven, they will be somewhat soft. Allow them to cool for a bit to get a crispy, crunchy, and more flavorful peanut.

1 PREHEAT the oven to 325°F.

2 IN a large bowl, combine all ingredients and mix well to coat the peanuts.

3 TRANSFER the coated peanuts from the bowl to a sheet pan and spread them out in a single layer.

4 BAKE for 40 minutes, removing the pan and stirring the peanuts around twice during cooking. Serve warm or at room temperature. Keep stored, non-refrigerated, in a sealed container.

APPS

Jackie's Yellow Squash Casserole

Calories: 220 | Fat: 19g | Protein: 8.5g | Fiber: 1g | **Net Carbs: 4g**

Rachel's sister Jackie always has a lot company! For years, we've been hearing our family rave about this casserole, but it wasn't until she brought it over that it truly became a tradition in our house. Now, if you're thinking you've tried them all or that squash is a boring old vegetable, you'll more than likely be surprised how this new outlook on a classic dish can truly bring a family together.

SHOPPING LIST

Kosher salt as needed

Vegetable oil spray

4–6 large yellow squash, sliced into ½-inch rounds

1 large Vidalia onion, cut in half and sliced thin

4 large eggs, beaten until frothy

8 ounces heavy cream or unsweetened soy milk

2 tablespoons mayonnaise

½ teaspoon kosher salt

¼ teaspoon black pepper

2 cups shredded Cheddar cheese

½ cup chopped pecans

HELPFUL HINTS

It's important to dry the par boiled squash and onions thoroughly or the casserole may be a bit soggy.

1 PREHEAT the oven to 350°F. Bring a large pot of water to a boil and season the water with salt. Spray a 13x9 inch baking dish with vegetable oil spray.

2 COOK the cut squash and onion in the boiling water until crisp-tender, about 5 minutes. Drain well and pat between several layers of paper towels to dry before transferring to the baking dish.

3 IN a bowl, mix the eggs, cream, mayonnaise, salt, and pepper to combine. Pour egg mixture over the par boiled squash and onion in the baking dish. Sprinkle the Cheddar cheese evenly over the top, pushing some of the cheese down into the squash mixture.

4 SPRINKLE the pecans evenly over HALF of the dish only (Jackie says that this is in case someone doesn't like nuts). Bake for 35 to 40 minutes, or until casserole just begins to brown.

APPS

Flourless Focaccia Bread

Calories: 165 | Fat: 8.5g | Protein: 12g | Fiber: 3g | **Net Carbs: 4.5g**

The Italian in me kept thinking about Focaccia Bread over the years and how I could bring it back into my low carb lifestyle. Now, here it is, baked until golden brown and topped with fresh herbs, onions, peppers, and Parmesan cheese. Though it's flourless and gluten-free—it's still just as delicious as ever!

SHOPPING LIST

Vegetable oil spray

CRUST

1 cup soy flour

¼ cup milled flax seed

3 large eggs

¾ cup half and half

⅓ cup club soda

1 teaspoon salt

TOPPINGS

¼ cup grated Parmesan cheese

⅓ cup julienned red bell peppers

⅓ cup julienned green bell peppers

⅓ cup julienned red onion

1 tablespoon chopped fresh rosemary leaves

¼ teaspoon minced fresh garlic

¼ teaspoon kosher salt

⅛ teaspoon black pepper

1 tablespoon extra-virgin olive oil

1 PLACE the oven rack in the center position and preheat to 375°F. Line a sheet pan with parchment paper and spray lightly with vegetable oil spray.

2 IN a medium bowl, stir together all of the crust ingredients to make a smooth, thick batter.

3 USING a rubber spatula, spread the batter as evenly as possible over the prepared sheet pan.

4 BAKE the crust for 20 to 22 minutes, until light golden brown and firm to the touch. Remove the crust from the oven and increase the oven temperature to 400°F.

5 EVENLY top crust with all of the topping ingredients, drizzling all with the olive oil, and return the pan to the oven. Bake for about 10 minutes more, until lightly browned. Remove and cut into 8 pieces before serving.

APPS

HELPFUL HINTS

While we prefer the flax seed, additional soy flour can be used in its place in a pinch.

Key West Crab Cakes with Mustard Sauce

Calories: 205 | Fat: 12g | Protein: 18g | Fiber: 1.5g | **Net Carbs: 5g**

My recipe for low carb crab cakes is an old favorite with my fans and the 4th highest rated recipe for any type of crab cake on Food Network's website (out of over 150 takes on the cakes). Well I've made them even better since they first appeared online and this recipe reflects those changes!

SHOPPING LIST

1 pound claw crabmeat

2 tablespoons finely diced red bell pepper

2 tablespoons finely diced green bell pepper

1 tablespoon mayonnaise

2 large eggs

2 tablespoons milled flax seed

1 tablespoon baking powder

1 tablespoon Worcestershire sauce

2 teaspoons Old Bay seasoning

2 tablespoons canola oil

MUSTARD SAUCE

¼ cup mayonnaise

¼ cup Dijon mustard

¼ teaspoon fresh lemon juice

1 IN a large bowl, mix all ingredients, except the canola oil and Mustard Sauce ingredients.

2 IN a separate bowl, combine all Mustard Sauce ingredients.

3 HEAT the canola oil in a large skillet over medium-high heat.

4 CAREFULLY spoon the batter in rounded tablespoons into the pan. (The resulting crab cakes will be the size of silver dollars, and the batter should be very loose. Once the egg in the batter starts to cook, the cakes will hold together fine)

5 COOK the crab cakes on one side until firm, about 2 minutes, and then flip and cook on the other side for about 1 more minute.

6 CONTINUE cooking in batches until you've used up all of the batter. Serve immediately with Mustard Sauce.

HELPFUL HINTS

The crabmeat used in this recipe can be found in cans or refrigerated tubs in your grocer's seafood department. Jumbo lump crabmeat is even better than the claw meat but nearly three times the price!

APPS

Guacamole

Calories: 120 | Fat: 11g | Protein: 1.5g | Fiber: 3.5g | **Net Carbs: 2g**

Avocados have to be one the best ingredients to keep around as they are loaded with vitamins and good fats - so much so that we've always got one or two ripening on our kitchen windowsill. We love turning them into guacamole as a dip for fresh vegetables or naturally low carb pork rinds or to simply serve over our Tequila Chicken (see page: 99).

APPS

SHOPPING LIST

1 ripe avocado (we prefer Hass)

⅓ cup sour cream

1 tablespoon chopped red onion

1 small clove garlic, minced

1 tablespoon finely chopped fresh cilantro leaves

1 teaspoon fresh lime juice

1 small pinch cayenne pepper

Salt and black pepper

1 CUT the avocado in half around the pit, twist it apart, and remove the pit.

2 USE a spoon to scoop the avocado pulp out of the skin, place in a medium bowl, and mash.

3 ADD all remaining ingredients and mix together until well blended.

4 COVER the surface of the guacamole with plastic wrap (to keep the dip from darkening due to air exposure) and refrigerate until ready to serve.

HELPFUL HINTS

Adding 2 diced tomatoes will make this into a fresh avocado salsa.

Rosemary Baked Olives

Calories: 30 | Fat: 2.5g | Protein: 0g | Fiber: 1g | **Net Carbs: 0.5g**

No matter what, I have to have an assortment of olives at any gathering or holiday dinner. It's a family tradition that dates back to before I was born. Roasting olives and serving them warm, as they are in this recipe, is a relatively new tradition of ours that really brings something new to the party.

SHOPPING LIST

2 cups large deli-style olives, mixed variety (green, black, Kalamata, etc.)

1 tablespoon fresh rosemary leaves, chopped

1 tablespoon lemon zest

⅛ teaspoon garlic powder

HELPFUL HINTS

Throw in some pepperoncini, roasted red peppers, marinated artichoke hearts, and thinly sliced fresh garlic for a loaded antipasti style olive mix.

1 PREHEAT the oven to 350°F.

2 ADD all ingredients to a small baking dish and toss to combine.

3 COVER with foil and bake for 25 minutes. Serve warm, garnished with fresh rosemary sprigs if desired.

APPS

Bacon-Wrapped Buffalo Shrimp Cocktail

Calories: 320 | Fat: 20g | Protein: 30g | Fiber: 1g | **Net Carbs: 4g**

A longtime fan of hot wings, I am equally taken by these delicate, easy-to-make appetizers. They're perfect for parties with a texture reminiscent of chicken, bursting with the same familiar flavors you love and looking all fancy in their bacon jackets—you'll find them difficult to stop popping in your mouth! Makes 30 pieces.

SHOPPING LIST

10 bacon slices

2 pounds peeled, deveined tail-on jumbo shrimp

30 wooden toothpicks

½ cup Louisiana hot sauce

¾ cup blue cheese dressing

4 celery ribs, cut into sticks

1 lemon, cut into 6 wedges

HELPFUL HINTS

You can also make these with sea scallops in place of the shrimp.

1 PREHEAT the oven to 400°F.

2 ARRANGE the bacon slices on a baking sheet, and bake until half-cooked, about 6 minutes. Let cool and cut each slice into thirds. Reserve the baking sheet; don't drain the fat.

3 STRETCH one-third of a bacon slice tightly around the center of each shrimp, securing with a toothpick.

4 ARRANGE the shrimp on the reserved baking sheet, and bake until just cooked through and the bacon is crispy, about 6 minutes more.

5 IMMEDIATELY transfer the shrimp to a bowl and gently toss with the hot sauce. To serve, pour the blue cheese dressing in a small serving bowl and place in the center of a serving platter, surrounded by the shrimp, celery sticks, and lemon wedges.

APPS

Teriyaki Ginger Chicken Satays

Calories: 170 | Fat: 8g | Protein: 22g | Fiber: 0g | **Net Carbs: 1g**

This recipe absolutely screams those Asian flavors we love, but what Rachel loves about these chicken thighs even more is how often they're on sale! These skewered bites of moist, flavorful poultry make for an excellent main course but also hold the power to kick-start any party! Makes 24 satays.

SHOPPING LIST

15 ounces teriyaki sauce (with no more than 2 grams sugar per serving)

6 tablespoons sesame oil

1 teaspoon minced fresh garlic

1 tablespoon minced fresh ginger

Juice of 1 lemon

1 tablespoon bulk sugar substitute (recommended: Splenda)

2 pounds boneless, skinless chicken thighs

1 tablespoon sesame seeds, toasted

24 bamboo skewers

HELPFUL HINTS

To toast sesame seeds, place a small skillet over heat until hot. Add the raw sesame seeds and gently stir with a wooden spoon, just until they begin to brown and pop. Let cool after removing from the heat.

1 COMBINE teriyaki sauce, sesame oil, garlic, ginger, lemon juice, and sugar substitute in a plastic or glass container large enough to hold all of the chicken.

2 CUT the chicken into twenty-four ½-inch-wide strips. Add to the marinade, cover, shake gently to mix, and refrigerate for at least 1 hour.

3 SOAK the bamboo skewers in water for 30 minutes to keep them from burning later.

4 PREHEAT the oven to 375°F.

5 THREAD 1 chicken strip onto each skewer, leaving about an inch of bamboo free at the blunt end, and line up on a baking sheet. Place in the oven and bake for about 20 minutes until fully cooked through. Sprinkle the skewers with toasted sesame seeds before serving.

APPS

Boston Baked Soy Beans

Calories: 110 | Fat: 6g | Protein: 9g | Fiber: 4.5g | **Net Carbs: 1.5g**

No crock pot or pressure cooker is needed here! All it takes is some bacon, and isn't that something that just makes everything better? We use black soy beans (available in the natural foods section of your grocery store) in place of regular beans to dramatically cut down on carbs.

SHOPPING LIST

2 slices thick-cut bacon, chopped

⅓ cup diced onion

½ teaspoon minced garlic

¼ cup tomato sauce

⅓ cup water

½ teaspoon dry mustard

¼ teaspoon beef base

¼ teaspoon kosher salt

⅛ teaspoon black pepper

3 tablespoons bulk sugar substitute (recommended: Splenda)

1 (15-oz) can organic soy beans, rinsed and drained

1 ADD the bacon pieces and onions to a sauce pan over medium-high heat and cook until bacon is nearly done.

2 STIR in the remaining ingredients, reduce the heat, and simmer for 10 minutes. Serve hot in a ceramic crock pot for presentation.

APPS

HELPFUL HINTS

If using thin slices of bacon instead of the thick-cut, simply use 3 or 4 for extra bulk.

Cheesy Cauliflower Fritters

Calories: 160 | Fat: 13g | Protein: 7.5g | Fiber: 1.5g | **Net Carbs: 3g**

Without the simple white, useless carbs that normally make up a fritter batter, you can go ahead and fry these veggie delights up without an ounce of regret! A true low carb favorite around our house, fritters come in all varieties; from Carnival cake, ham and Swiss, or even clam fritters, this is a must have for your arsenal of low carb comfort foods! Makes about 24 fritters.

SHOPPING LIST

1 cup cauliflower, coarsely chopped

4 to 6 cups vegetable oil

½ cup shredded sharp Cheddar cheese

¼ cup grated Parmesan cheese

1 cup soy flour

¼ cup milled flax seed

3 large eggs

1 tablespoon baking powder

½ teaspoon kosher salt

¼ teaspoon black pepper

¼ teaspoon onion powder

1 BRING a small pot of water to a boil. Season the water with salt and cook the chopped cauliflower in the boiling water until crisp-tender, about 3 minutes. Drain well and pat between several layers of paper towels to dry, and set aside.

2 PLACE a pot over medium-high heat and fill with at least 3 inches of vegetable oil. Heat oil until about 350°F, about 5 minutes (a candy thermometer works well for this, or use an electric portable deep fryer).

3 IN a large bowl, combine cauliflower and all remaining ingredients and mix well (If too thick, thin with a couple tablespoons of water).

4 USING a teaspoon, drop walnut sized amounts of the batter gently into the hot oil, being careful not to splash.

5 FRY the fritters in small batches of 4 or 5 for about 3 minutes each batch, or until deep golden brown. Let rest on paper towels to drain excess oil before serving hot.

HELPFUL HINTS

Try adding different fillings in place of the cauliflower such as zucchini, broccoli, or my favorite—broccoli with diced ham and Gruyere cheese!

APPS

Roasted Chipotle Seeds and Nuts

Calories: 130 | Fat: 12g | Protein: 3.5g | Fiber: 2g | **Net Carbs: 1g**

Rachel's been known to keep a bag of seeds and nuts in her purse, and it's not out of the ordinary for me to find a zip lock container of them tucked away in my carry-on when I travel. While you can't bring salmon on a plane, you can still get a healthy dose of omega 3 fatty acids, which walnuts are loaded with, and potassium from the sunflower seeds, which is a natural weapon against fighting muscle cramps.

SHOPPING LIST

1 cup raw almonds

1 cup pecan halves

1 cup walnut halves

½ cup unsalted shelled sunflower seeds

4 tablespoons butter, melted

½ teaspoon dried thyme

½ teaspoon dried cilantro

½ teaspoon kosher salt

½ teaspoon garlic powder

½ teaspoon chili powder

½ teaspoon ground cumin

¼ teaspoon crushed dried chipotle pepper (see hints)

¼ teaspoon Italian seasoning

2 pinches of cayenne pepper

1 PREHEAT the oven to 350°F.

2 IN a large bowl, combine the nuts, seeds, melted butter, and all of the seasonings. Toss to coat well.

3 SPREAD the coated nuts in a single layer on a baking sheet and bake for 15 to 20 minutes. Shake the pan every few minutes while cooking to make sure the nuts cook evenly on all sides.

4 REMOVE from the oven and let cool. Store leftovers unrefrigerated in an airtight container.

HELPFUL HINTS

Tobasco brand hot sauce makes a chipotle version, which works great if you can't find the crushed chipotle peppers.

Canadian Steak Seasoning

Calories: 5 | Fat: 0g | Protein: 0g | Fiber: 0g | **Net Carbs: 0g**

This is my take on a famous store-bought steak seasoning with a Canadian city in the name. Although it is mostly used on steaks, this seasoning has been the secret ingredient for my world-famous chicken wings found on the menu of every restaurant I've ever opened! In fact, I like to use this on just about everything—even vegetables. Making it yourself ensures that you've got all the flavor without any of the hidden sugars or starches that store-bought seasoning mixes notoriously contain! Makes about ½ cup.

SHOPPING LIST

3 tablespoons paprika

2 tablespoons kosher salt

1 tablespoon coarse black pepper

1 tablespoon granulated garlic

1 tablespoon onion powder

1 tablespoon crushed coriander

1 tablespoon dill weed

1 teaspoon crushed red pepper

1 COMBINE all ingredients, mixing well, and store in an airtight container or spice canister.

APPS

HELPFUL HINTS

Coriander is from the top of the cilantro plant and may be substituted with dried cilantro leaves. Always check the ethnic food section of your grocery store for hard to find spices. I find that their prices on everyday spices are far less expensive too.

Five-Spice Candied Almonds

Calories: 100 | Fat: 7.5g | Protein: 4g | Fiber: 2g | **Net Carbs: 3g**

I can tell you that your house will come alive with comforting aromas as these tasty morsels roast. Seasoned with cinnamon, allspice, and ginger, these almonds are a healthy and Far East twist on the more traditional roasted nuts found at carnivals and festivals. Great for the holidays or as an anytime cravings buster!

SHOPPING LIST

Vegetable oil spray

1 large egg white

1 ½ teaspoons water

¾ cup bulk sugar substitute (recommended: Splenda)

⅛ teaspoon ground cinnamon

⅛ teaspoon ground allspice

⅛ teaspoon ground ginger

⅛ teaspoon ground nutmeg

⅛ teaspoon ground cloves

2 cups whole raw almonds

HELPFUL HINTS

For more traditional candied almonds, simply add ½ teaspoon vanilla extract and substitute only ½ teaspoon ground cinnamon in place of all five spices in this recipe. Walnuts and pecan halves can also be used with or in place of the almonds.

1 PREHEAT oven to 325°F.

2 CUT a brown paper bag to size and use it to line a cookie sheet. Spray the top surface of the paper heavily with cooking spray.

3 WHISK the egg white in a bowl until frothy. Add the water, sugar substitute, and spices, and whisk thoroughly.

4 ADD the almonds to the egg white mixture and toss to coat well.

5 SPREAD the coated nuts in a single layer on the oil-coated paper and bake for 20 to 25 minutes. Allow to cool at least 10 minutes before breaking apart and storing in a sealed container at room temperature.

APPS

Ham and Pear California Rolls

Calories: 170 | Fat: 12g | Protein: 7g | Fiber: 2g | **Net Carbs: 7g**

Since I do enjoy sushi, especially California rolls, I've used them as inspiration when coming up with this very fresh, very easy appetizer. Done much in the way of sushi rolls and using ingredients you'd usually find on an antipasti platter, think of it as Italian sushi!

SHOPPING LIST

8 ounces cream cheese, softened to room temperature

½ pound thinly sliced deli ham, at least 8 slices

2 ripe bartlet pears, sliced into thin wedges (may use any pear)

1 cup fresh baby arugula, may use fresh spinach

HELPFUL HINTS

Using prosciutto in place of the ham and mascarpone cheese (a creamy Italian cheese) in place of the regular cream cheese turns the gourmet dial on this recipe up an extra notch!

1 SPREAD a thin layer of the cream cheese over each slice of ham to start the rolls.

2 PLACE a couple of pear slices in the center of each roll lengthwise and top with a few sprigs of arugula.

3 ROLL the ham up around the fillings and place on a plate, seam-side down.

4 REFRIGERATE rolls for 30 minutes until cheese is firm. Cut each roll on a bias or slight slant into 3 slices. Serve chilled rolls atop a bed of baby arugula.

APPS

Ginger Tea

Calories: 10 | Fat: 0g | Protein: 0g | Fiber: 0g | **Net Carbs: 1g**

Rachel is a big fan of ginger; for years, she's been sneaking it into our chicken soup. This root isn't just good for you, but it also has a flavor all its own and is easily hidden in just about anything!

SHOPPING LIST

2 ½ cups water

2 tablespoons fresh ginger root, peeled and chopped

1 teaspoon fresh lime juice

1 ½ tablespoons bulk sugar substitute (recommended: Splenda)

HELPFUL HINTS

To keep any leftover ginger root from drying out, I always wrap it in a damp paper towel before sealing in a plastic bag and refrigerating.

1 ADD the water and ginger to a small pot over medium-high heat and simmer for about 6 minutes.

2 REMOVE from heat, add all remaining ingredients, and serve hot!

APPS

White Wine Sangria

Calories: 45 | Fat: 0g | Protein: 0g | Fiber: 0g | **Net Carbs: 2g**

My wife and I enjoy this refreshing take on a Mexican favorite on hot summer days by our pool. It's also absolutely perfect for when you're standing in front of a blazing hot grill (as I usually am)!

SHOPPING LIST

2 cups dry Chardonnay, Chablis, or Pinot Grigio wine

2 cups club soda or seltzer water (may use diet lemon lime soda)

¼ cup fresh lime juice

¼ cup fresh lemon juice

4 packets sugar substitute (recommended: Splenda)

1 lemon, sliced into discs

1 lime, sliced into discs

1 Mix all the ingredients together in a punch bowl. Serve immediately poured into glasses over ice.

HELPFUL HINTS

Alcohol can inhibit weight loss in some people, so you may want to enjoy drinks like this in moderation.

APPS

POULTRY

Spinach and Artichoke Stuffed Chicken

Calories: 260 | Fat: 10.5g | Protein: 34g | Fiber: 3g | **Net Carbs: 3g**

Everyone loves a stuffed chicken breast, but in the old days it wasn't my favorite to make. It was a lot of work between the stuffing, breading, freezing to hold the shape, frying, and then finally finishing in the oven! I get tired just thinking about that process and how messy it was. This much easier, low carb version avoids the breading and frying, cutting the prep time in half.

SHOPPING LIST

2 tablespoons extra virgin olive oil

4 boneless, skinless chicken breasts

½ teaspoon kosher salt

¼ teaspoon black pepper

½ teaspoon Italian seasoning

2 teaspoons minced garlic

¼ cup Parmesan cheese

1 cup frozen chopped spinach, thawed and drained

6 ounces marinated artichoke hearts, drained and chopped

¼ cup diced roasted red peppers

PREHEAT the oven to 400°F and grease a sheet pan with the olive oil.

POUND the chicken breasts until about ⅓ inch thick at all parts. The easiest and cleanest way to do this is to place them into a food storage bag one at a time, close the bag, and pound with a mallet, heavy rolling pin, or frying pan.

PLACE pounded chicken breasts on the oiled sheet pan and cover with salt, pepper, and Italian seasoning. Flip chicken breasts in the oil on the pan to coat well and disperse the seasoning to both sides.

In a mixing bowl, combine garlic, Parmesan cheese, spinach, artichoke hearts, and roasted peppers.

Flip breasts, so the overlapping ends are down and bake 20 minutes, or until chicken is thoroughly cooked through and slicing into one reveals no pink.

Spoon an equal amount of the filling down the center of each chicken breast lengthwise, packing it in a neat row for easier rolling.

Serve sliced in half diagonally, garnished with fresh basil or parsley sprigs, if desired.

HELPFUL HINTS

For parties, you can slice each stuffed chicken breast into pinwheels and make a platter!

Roll the sides of the chicken breasts up and over the filling, until overlapping.

Buffalo Baked Chicken with Gorgonzola Cream Sauce

Calories: 535 | Fat: 32g | Protein: 55g | Fiber: 1g | **Net Carbs: 4g**

This is one of my absolute favorites of all of the new recipes in this book. You get all of the flavors of hot wings with bleu cheese dressing in a much more dinner-appropriate form. While the pork rinds may seem unusual, they crisp the chicken breasts up in the oven without deep-frying.

SHOPPING LIST

Vegetable oil spray

1 large bag (about 4 ounces) regular pork rinds

½ teaspoon Italian seasoning

¼ teaspoon black pepper

⅛ teaspoon garlic powder

1 ½ pounds thin chicken breast cutlets

2 large eggs, beaten in a bowl

¼ cup Louisiana hot sauce

¼ cup butter, melted

GORGONZOLA CREAM SAUCE

⅔ cup gorgonzola or any bleu cheese

¼ cup mayonnaise

Dash of Worcestershire sauce

¼ teaspoon black pepper

HELPFUL HINTS

Don't let the cooked chicken sit in the hot sauce and butter mixture too long or it will become soggy.

POULTRY

1 PREHEAT the oven to 375°F and spray a sheet pan with vegetable oil spray.

2 ADD the pork rinds, Italian seasoning, pepper, and garlic powder to a large food storage bag and use a rolling pin or heavy can to crush the rinds until smooth.

3 ONE at a time, dip each chicken cutlet first into the beaten egg and then into the bag of seasoned pork rinds, shaking to coat.

4 PLACE the coated chicken breast cutlets in a single layer on the greased sheet pan and bake for 25 to 30 minutes until the chicken is thoroughly cooked through.

5 MEANWHILE, in a mixing bowl, combine the hot sauce and melted butter and set aside.

6 A few minutes before the chicken is done cooking, add all Gorgonzola Cream Sauce ingredients to a small pan over medium heat. Stir constantly for 4 to 5 minutes, just until the gorgonzola melts and all ingredients are combined.

7 WHEN the chicken is finished cooking, remove from oven and quickly toss each piece in the bowl of hot sauce and butter to coat well before serving draped with the warm Gorgonzola Cream Sauce. Serve with celery sticks, if desired.

Tequila Chicken

Calories: 370 | Fat: 20g | Protein: 38g | Fiber: 0.5g | **Net Carbs: 2g**

If you were beginning to think chicken was getting old and boring, think again, because this recipe is sure to ignite your taste buds! Rachel and I love this dish so much that we even made it the first time we appeared on television!

SHOPPING LIST

Vegetable oil spray

2 tablespoons extra-virgin olive oil

4 boneless, skinless chicken breasts

2 tablespoons tequila

2 tablespoons chopped red onion

2 tablespoons chopped fresh cilantro

¼ teaspoon minced fresh garlic

1 ½ tablespoons ground cumin

½ teaspoon kosher salt

¼ teaspoon black pepper

⅛ teaspoon cayenne pepper

4 ounces shredded Colby or Cheddar-jack cheese

4 tablespoons sour cream

4 tablespoons salsa picante

1 PREHEAT oven to 400°F. Spray a sheet pan with vegetable oil and set aside.

2 PLACE the olive oil, the chicken breast fillets, and all other ingredients, except the cheese, sour cream, and salsa, into a bowl. Toss until coated.

3 PLACE the coated filets on the baking sheet and bake for 25 to 30 minutes, or until a meat thermometer inserted into the thickest piece of chicken registers at least 165°F.

4 REMOVE the cooked chicken from the oven, top with the shredded cheese, and return to the oven just long enough for the cheese to melt, about 2 minutes.

5 SERVE each piece topped with 1 tablespoon each of the sour cream and salsa.

POULTRY

HELPFUL HINTS

While the alcohol cooks out of this, you can leave the tequila out altogether if desired.

Chicken Newburg

Calories: 430 | Fat: 23g | Protein: 53g | Fiber: 2.5g | **Net Carbs: 5g**

When I was just starting out as a chef in the 70's, French Continental and Nouvelle cuisines were all the rage. Newburg, usually made with lobster, was as common on a menu as cheeseburgers are today! Of course, lobster can be pricey nowadays, but this chicken breast recipe still dishes up all those wonderful flavors of the past without breaking the bank.

POULTRY

SHOPPING LIST

2 tablespoons extra virgin olive oil

2 pounds boneless, skinless chicken breasts

1 cup sliced yellow onion

8 ounces sliced button mushrooms

2 tablespoons paprika

½ teaspoon kosher salt

¼ teaspoon black pepper

½ cup chicken broth

2 ounces cream sherry (may use balsamic vinegar)

8 ounces sour cream or Greek yogurt

Chopped fresh chives, for garnish

1 PLACE oil in a large skillet over medium-high heat.

2 ADD chicken and lightly brown on each side, about 1 to 2 minutes per side.

3 LOWER the heat to medium and stir in onions, mushrooms, paprika, salt, and pepper, allowing to cook 2 additional minutes.

4 POUR in the chicken broth and sherry. Cover and simmer for 8 to 10 minutes, until chicken is thoroughly cooked and cutting into the thickest piece reveals no pink.

5 REMOVE from heat and stir in sour cream. Serve immediately, garnished with a sprinkle of paprika and chopped chives if desired.

HELPFUL HINTS

You can also turn this recipe into a low carb seafood version. Simply replace the chicken with 1 pound of shrimp, crab, or BOTH, and simmer for only 4 minutes. Serve over spaghetti squash.

Chicken with Pistachio Pesto

Calories: 390 | Fat: 26g | Protein: 33g | Fiber: 1g | **Net Carbs: 2g**

Pesto can truly breathe new life into poultry, especially when you replace the usual pine nuts with pistachios! Fresh basil leaves, Parmesan, and garlic bring traditional flavors to the table, but who says the nutty flavor has to stay the same—nothing should ever be limited when you're living a low carb lifestyle.

SHOPPING LIST

⅓ cup + 2 teaspoons olive oil

¼ cup shelled pistachios

1 cup basil leaves, packed

1 clove garlic

¼ cup grated Parmesan cheese

4 boneless, skinless chicken breasts

Salt and pepper

HELPFUL HINTS

Feel free to use pecans, almonds, walnuts, or even the traditional pine nuts in place of the pistachios to change up the flavor each time you make this recipe!

1 PREHEAT the oven to 375°F and grease a sheet pan with the 2 teaspoons olive oil.

2 PLACE remaining ⅓ cup olive oil, pistachios, basil leaves, garlic, and Parmesan cheese in a food processor and pulse until almost entirely puréed but still grainy.

3 PLACE the chicken breasts on the greased sheet pan and generously season with salt and pepper.

4 TOP each breast with an equal amount of pesto purée, spreading to cover evenly.

5 BAKE for 25 to 30 minutes, or until cutting into the thickest piece reveals no pink and juices run clear. Serve garnished with fresh basil, if desired.

POULTRY

Rotisserie Chicken Stew and Dumplings

Calories: 200 | Fat: 7g | Protein: 25g | Fiber: 5g | **Net Carbs: 4.5g**

Did someone say "chicken and dumplings" in a low carb cookbook? Yes, I did! This recipe is a simple and quick way to get your comfort on. I am sure you've realized by now that I just love finding new ways to use the delicious and inexpensive supermarket rotisserie chickens!

SHOPPING LIST

CHICKEN STEW

8 cups chicken stock or broth

2 cups diced cooked chicken (rotisserie chicken leftovers are perfect)

½ white onion, peeled and quartered

3 stalks celery, cut into large chunks

2 bay leaves

½ teaspoon poultry seasoning

1 teaspoon chopped fresh parsley

Salt and pepper

DUMPLINGS

1 cup soy flour

¼ cup milled flax seed

2 large eggs

½ cup water

¼ teaspoon kosher salt

⅛ teaspoon black pepper

1 ADD all of the chicken stew ingredients to a large stock pot and bring to a slow simmer for 5 minutes. Add salt and pepper to taste.

2 MEANWHILE, in a medium bowl, combine the dumpling ingredients, mixing well with a rubber spatula. Add more water if needed until the consistency is that of a gooey dough.

3 USING 2 regular tablespoons, drop scant tablespoons of the mixture into the hot stew using one spoon to scrape the mixture off of the other.

4 LET the dumplings simmer for 10 minutes before serving.

POULTRY

HELPFUL HINTS

I prefer to use chicken base to make the chicken stock in my recipes (whenever I don't have any homemade stock on hand).

Pesto Chicken Parmesan

Calories: 490 | Fat: 31g | Protein: 47g | Fiber: 0g | **Net Carbs: 5g**

Naturally low in carbs as well as a great way to add flavor, pesto has certainly become one of our favorite uses for all the basil plants on our patio. Fresh pesto keeps for days when refrigerated (can also be frozen), and complements not just chicken but a variety of proteins. Cheese, for example, certainly—as it usually does—kicks the palette into high gear.

SHOPPING LIST

Vegetable oil spray

2–3 pounds boneless, skinless chicken breasts

2 cups shredded mozzarella cheese

1 cup diced tomatoes

PESTO

2 packed cups fresh basil leaves

½ cup extra virgin olive oil

3 tablespoons pine nuts, toasted in a dry skillet over medium heat until lightly browned

1 small garlic clove

¼ teaspoon kosher salt

¼ teaspoon black pepper

½ cup grated Parmesan cheese

HELPFUL HINTS

When we don't have pine nuts, we love to use shelled sunflower seeds to make this homemade pesto.

1 PREHEAT the oven to 375°F and spray a sheet pan with vegetable oil.

2 PLACE all of the pesto ingredients into a food processor or blender and pulse on high until almost puréed.

3 ARRANGE the chicken breasts in a single layer on the sheet pan and spread each piece with a generous amount of pesto on top.

4 BAKE for about 30 minutes, until the chicken is completely cooked and a meat thermometer stuck in the thickest piece reads 165°F.

5 REMOVE cooked chicken, top each with mozzarella, and return to the oven for 5 additional minutes, or until cheese is melted.

6 REMOVE chicken a final time and sprinkle each piece with diced tomatoes before serving garnished with fresh basil, if desired.

POULTRY

Mediterranean Chicken

Calories: 640 | Fat: 33g | Protein: 75g | Fiber: 3g | **Net Carbs: 4g**

These breaded chicken cutlets are topped with artichoke hearts and roasted red peppers, which are classic Mediterranean ingredients. Then I top that with cheese, because it only gets better with cheese!

POULTRY

SHOPPING LIST

Vegetable oil spray

1 (4-ounce) bag pork rinds

¼ cup grated Parmesan cheese

½ teaspoon Italian seasoning

¼ teaspoon black pepper

⅛ teaspoon garlic powder

1 ½ pounds boneless, skinless chicken breasts, cut or pounded into thin cutlets

2 large eggs, beaten in a bowl

1 (6-ounce) jar marinated artichoke hearts, drained and chopped

1 (8-ounce) jar roasted red peppers, cut into strips

2 cups shredded Monterey Jack cheese

HELPFUL HINTS

You can also make this recipe without breading the chicken in pork rinds. Simply season the bare chicken with the Parmesan cheese and spices instead and skip the eggs.

1 PREHEAT the oven to 375°F and spray a 9x13 baking dish with vegetable oil spray.

2 ADD the pork rinds, Parmesan cheese, Italian seasoning, pepper, and garlic powder to a large food storage bag and use a rolling pin or heavy can to crush the rinds smooth.

3 ONE at a time, dip each chicken cutlet into the beaten egg and then into the bag of seasoned pork rinds, shaking to coat.

4 PLACE the coated chicken breast cutlets in a single layer in the greased baking dish. Top each evenly with the marinated artichokes and roasted peppers.

5 BAKE 25 to 30 minutes, until chicken is thoroughly cooked and cutting into a piece at its thickest part reveals no pink.

6 TOP cooked chicken breasts with the shredded cheese and return to the oven for 5 minutes more, just until cheese is bubbly. Serve immediately garnished with sliced Kalamata or black olives, if desired.

Lemon Garlic Chicken

Calories: 440 | Fat: 19g | Protein: 63g | Fiber: 0g | **Net Carbs: 0g**

Lemon and garlic are two of the most essential staples in cooking, especially when you're cooking chicken! I like to think that this simple recipe for a whole roasted chicken is as essential as the ingredients themselves.

SHOPPING LIST

Vegetable oil spray

2 tablespoons olive oil

2 tablespoons fresh lemon juice

1 teaspoon fresh lemon zest

2 cloves garlic, crushed

¼ teaspoon garlic powder

½ teaspoon kosher salt

¼ teaspoon black pepper

3 ½ -4 pound whole fresh chicken

¼ teaspoon paprika

HELPFUL HINTS

Baste the chicken occasionally during cooking for the best result. Also, try squeezing fresh lemon juice over each piece before serving to heighten the flavor even further!

1 PREHEAT the oven to 350°F and spray a large roasting pan with vegetable oil spray.

2 IN a mixing bowl, whisk together the oil, lemon juice, lemon zest, garlic, garlic powder, salt, and pepper to create a rub.

3 PLACE the chicken breast-up in the roasting pan, spread the rub evenly over the entire bird, and then sprinkle with paprika.

4 BAKE the chicken for 75 to 90 minutes, until an instant-read thermometer stuck in the thickest piece registers 165°F.

5 LET rest for 10 minutes before cutting to serve basted in the juices from the pan and garnished with chopped fresh parsley and slices of lemon, if desired.

POULTRY

Chicken Stella Scarpariello

Calories: 445 | Fat: 26g | Protein: 45g | Fiber: 1.5g | **Net Carbs: 3g**

This Italian classic was a staple in my relatives' houses growing up; though their version more resembled a kitchen sink stew. Italian sausage and chicken were always staples, while throwing in whatever vegetables were on hand was common practice. The real beauty of this chockfull hearty recipe is that there are so many flavors involved that I don't even miss the pasta!

SHOPPING LIST

¼ cup extra virgin olive oil

1 pound mild or hot Italian sausage, cut into 2-inch lengths

2 pounds boneless, skinless chicken thighs, each piece cut into thirds

1 medium yellow onion, quartered and separated into rings

3 bell peppers (any color), cut into 1-inch wide strips

1 cup chicken stock

½ cup balsamic vinegar

2 teaspoons minced garlic

2 tablespoons chopped fresh basil

1 teaspoon dried oregano

½ teaspoon kosher salt

¼ teaspoon crushed red pepper flakes

¼ teaspoon black pepper

8 ounces small button mushrooms

4 marinated hot cherry peppers, halved

1 PREHEAT the oven to 375°F.

2 HEAT 2 tablespoons of the oil in a large skillet over medium-high heat. Add the sausage and chicken, and then cook, stirring occasionally, until browned, about 5 minutes.

3 DRAIN the fat from the skillet (the meat does not have to be fully cooked at this point as it will finish cooking in the oven).

4 MEANWHILE, heat the remaining 2 tablespoons of oil in a separate large skillet over medium-high heat. Add the onions and peppers and cook for about 2 minutes, just until tender.

5 ADD the browned meat, cooked onions and peppers, and all remaining ingredients to a casserole dish, tossing to combine.

6 BAKE uncovered for about 40 minutes. Serve garnished with fresh basil, lemon slices, and shaved Parmesan cheese, if desired.

POULTRY

HELPFUL HINTS

Turkey sausage and boneless chicken breast may be substituted to significantly reduce the fat in this recipe.

Grilled Mojito Chicken

Calories: 300 | Fat: 9g | Protein: 48.5g | Fiber: 1g | **Net Carbs: 2.5g**

Mint is the main ingredient (besides rum!) in a classic Caribbean Mojito, and this past summer we "muddled" our way through our share of mint as our pool patio herb garden grew out of control. Besides enjoying refreshing drinks by the pool, we also came up with this wonderful marinated chicken breast recipe that is fit to serve a pirate (Caribbean joke). Do you not have pirates where you live? All jokes aside, we live about 5 minutes from Disney World, so we are pretty darn close to some Caribbean pirates!

SHOPPING LIST

6 boneless, skinless chicken breasts

½ cup lime juice

¼ cup rum (may use sherry vinegar or red wine vinegar)

2 tablespoons vegetable oil

½ cup mint leaves, finely chopped

¼ cup bulk sugar substitute (recommended: Splenda)

1 tablespoon grated lime zest

1 clove fresh garlic, minced

1 tablespoon ground cumin

½ teaspoon onion powder

½ teaspoon cayenne pepper, optional

2 teaspoons kosher salt

½ teaspoon black pepper

POULTRY

1 PLACE the chicken breasts in a 1-gallon food storage bag or plastic container.

2 WHISK together all remaining ingredients and pour over the chicken in the bag. Seal or cover, and refrigerate for 2 hours before cooking. (Do not marinate overnight when using lime juice as it will cook and break down the meat.)

3 ONCE chicken is marinated, build a charcoal fire or preheat a gas grill or grill pan to high. Remove the chicken from the bag and discard the used marinade.

4 PLACE the chicken breasts on the grill and cook about 10 minutes on each side, or until an instant-read thermometer stuck in the thickest piece reads 165°F. Serve garnished with lime and sprigs of mint.

HELPFUL HINTS

The marinade in this recipe works great for pork or seafood as well. For extra-large or very thick chicken breasts, simply filet them in half and they will both marinate and cook in about ½ the time.

Low Carb Southern Fried Chicken

Calories: 425 | Fat: 20g | Protein: 50g | Fiber: 3.5g | **Net Carbs: 4g**

Growing up in the South, fried chicken was not only a staple but also a comfort food for me. As a matter of fact, it still is to this day! Take that flour and forget about it, because seasoned soy flour crisps up so nicely that it'll never leave you feeling far from home.

SHOPPING LIST

3 to 6 cups vegetable oil, for frying

3 large eggs

¼ cup heavy cream, may use water

2 ⅓ cups soy flour

2 teaspoons salt

1 teaspoon black pepper

1 teaspoon garlic powder

1 teaspoon poultry seasoning

1 whole chicken, cut into 8 pieces, or 3 pounds boneless chicken breasts

Salt and black pepper

HELPFUL HINTS

Ask your grocery store's butcher to cut a whole chicken into the breasts, thighs, wings, and legs if you don't feel confident enough to do it yourself.

1 PREHEAT the oven to 350°F. Place a deep, heavy pot over medium-high heat and fill with at least 2 inches of vegetable oil. Heat the oil to 350°F. It's very important to monitor and maintain the temperature as the soy flour breading, as well as your oil, can burn.

2 IN a medium bowl, mix the eggs and cream to make an egg wash. In a larger bowl, mix all the breading ingredients together.

3 SEASON the chicken well with salt and pepper. Dip each piece first in the breading, then in the egg wash, and then back in the breading again, making sure to coat well on all sides. Shake off any excess breading.

4 CAREFULLY place the chicken pieces in the hot oil using a slotted spatula or spoon (wear mitts, please!) and fry until golden brown and crisp— usually just a few minutes is enough.

5 REMOVE the chicken pieces and drain on paper towels.

6 PLACE the chicken pieces on a baking sheet. Because the soy flour browns long before the chicken is cooked, it's best to finish the chicken by baking in the oven. Bake 20 to 25 minutes. A meat thermometer inserted into the thickest part of the chicken should register at least 165°F. Serve immediately.

POULTRY

Turkey Stroganoff

Calories: 305 | Fat: 19.5g | Protein: 30g | Fiber: 1g | **Net Carbs: 2.5g**

With dishes like this noodle-less take on a familiar classic, it goes to show that living a low carb lifestyle doesn't necessarily mean you have to throw all those old recipes in the garbage bin! Of course, it's also another example of a dish that never needed to sit atop a bed of carbs in the first place. Trust me, you'll feel good about losing your noodles!

SHOPPING LIST

2 tablespoons vegetable oil

2 cups chopped celery

⅓ cup chopped red onion

2 ½ pounds ground turkey

8 ounces sliced Baby Bella or button mushrooms

¼ teaspoon minced fresh garlic

1 teaspoon dried tarragon

1 ½ teaspoons salt

¼ teaspoon black pepper

¼ teaspoon garlic powder

1 cup sour cream

2 tablespoons sliced scallions

1 HEAT the oil in a large skillet over medium-high heat. Add the celery and onion, and cook until slightly tender.

2 ADD the ground turkey and cook until browned. Drain off the excess fat with a spoon or turkey baster.

3 ADD the mushrooms, garlic, and seasonings, and simmer for 4 to 5 minutes, stirring constantly.

4 REMOVE from the heat, stir in the sour cream, and serve garnished with the scallion tops.

HELPFUL HINTS

I like to serve this over cooked spaghetti squash. My Anaheim Shrimp Scampi recipe (see page: 144) includes step by step directions for preparing spaghetti squash.

POULTRY

Easy Cheesy Chili Chicken

Calories: 455 | Fat: 20g | Protein: 70g | Fiber: 2g | **Net Carbs: 3g**

When my best friend Jimi and I threw this recipe together in between writing my first and second cookbooks, I had no idea that this would go on to become one of my all-time most popular recipes. What started out as a challenge in cooking with the few ingredients we had on hand is now a true Stella Style classic!

SHOPPING LIST

2 tablespoons extra virgin olive oil

2 tablespoons chopped cilantro, plus a few whole leaves, for garnish

1 tablespoon chili powder

1 tablespoon ground cumin

2 teaspoons kosher salt

1 clove garlic, minced

½ teaspoon black pepper

⅛ teaspoon cayenne pepper

2 pounds boneless, skinless chicken breast

¼ cup julienned green bell pepper

2 tablespoons diced red onion

¼ cup cored and diced plum tomatoes

4 ounces shredded Colby-Jack cheese

1 PREHEAT the oven to 400°F. Line a sheet pan with aluminum foil.

2 WHISK together the oil, chopped cilantro, chili powder, cumin, salt, garlic, pepper, and cayenne pepper in a bowl. Add the chicken to the bowl and toss to coat.

3 TRANSFER the coated chicken to the foil-lined baking sheet and arrange the green pepper, onion, and tomatoes evenly over each.

4 ROAST until the largest piece is just cooked through and an instant-read thermometer inserted in the thickest part reads 165°F, about 20 minutes.

5 REMOVE the chicken from the oven and immediately top with the cheese. Serve as the cheese melts, garnished with fresh cilantro leaves.

POULTRY

HELPFUL HINTS

Though olive oil is a "good" fat, you can lower the fat in this recipe by cutting the oil down to only 1 tablespoon. You can also use less of an extra-sharp Cheddar cheese in place of the Colby-Jack to further reduce the fat without sacrificing flavor.

Family-Style Chicken

Calories: 250 | Fat: 11g | Protein: 35g | Fiber: 0g | **Net Carbs: 1g**

My Family-Style Chicken may take a little time to cook, but I promise you that it literally falls right off the bone. For Rachel and I, this brings back fond memories of Wright's Farm, a family-style restaurant in Rhode Island. They make the best family-style chicken on the planet, but I'd like to think that mine is a very, very close second!

SHOPPING LIST

Vegetable oil spray

1 (4-pound) chicken, cut into 8 pieces

1 teaspoon kosher salt

1 teaspoon paprika

½ teaspoon black pepper

½ teaspoon poultry seasoning

½ teaspoon dried oregano

⅛ teaspoon garlic powder

4 bay leaves

Lemon zest, for garnish

Chopped parsley, for garnish

HELPFUL HINTS

Make this a full meal by following the preparation for Simply Roasted Vegetables (see page: 178) and adding them to the roasting pan with the chicken for the last 35 minutes of baking.

1 PREHEAT the oven to 350°F. Lightly coat a roasting pan with vegetable oil spray.

2 PLACE the chicken pieces in the center of the pan and sprinkle each piece evenly with the remaining ingredients, excluding the garnishes.

3 COVER the pan tightly with aluminum foil and bake for 1 hour.

4 REMOVE the chicken from the oven and baste with the drippings. Continue baking uncovered until well browned, about 1 additional hour, or until the meat is falling off the bones.

5 ARRANGE the chicken on a platter and sprinkle with lemon zest and chopped parsley before serving.

POULTRY

Herb Rub

Calories: 110 | Fat: 11g | Protein: 0g | Fiber: 0g | **Net Carbs: 1g**

Fresh herbs are one of my favorite things! Rachel started keeping a few plants, which grew into a full-blown garden in our backyard. Since then, we have more of the goodness than we know what to do with, which is why I rely on this Herb Rub to keep the natural flavors going for weeks and my time prepping to a minimum.

SHOPPING LIST

½ cup fresh cilantro leaves, stemmed and washed

½ cup fresh basil leaves, stemmed and washed

½ cup fresh flat-leaf parsley, stemmed and washed

¼ cup extra virgin olive oil

¼ cup canola oil

2 tablespoons kosher salt

1 tablespoon paprika

1 ½ teaspoons black pepper

2 teaspoons garlic powder

2 teaspoons onion powder

1 PLACE all ingredients in a food processor and blend on high for about 1 minute, until well combined.

2 REMOVE and refrigerate for as long as 3 weeks in a plastic or glass container (metal containers may turn the herbs brown).

HELPFUL HINTS

If you'd like to cut back on the oil, try using half the amount, which will make for a thicker rub easily thinned by a bit of water just before use.

POULTRY

Herb-Roasted Chicken Breasts

Calories: 360 | Fat: 10g | Protein: 65g | Fiber: .5g | **Net Carbs: .5g**

Chicken is often put on sale at our grocery store, which is the perfect time to stock up! And just to keep up with the overflow of all that poultry, we started our herb garden so that we can have plenty of that Herb Rub around!

SHOPPING LIST

Vegetable oil spray

3 tablespoons Herb Rub (see recipe at left)

2 ½ pounds boneless, skinless chicken breasts

Lemon slices, for garnish

Fresh herbs, for garnish

HELPFUL HINTS

We often prepare these on the grill (though that wouldn't qualify them as "roasted" anymore). Simply grill for about 6 minutes on each side, or until cutting into the thickest piece reveals no pink.

1 PREHEAT the oven to 400°F. Spray a sheet pan with vegetable oil.

2 PLACE the Herb Rub and chicken breasts into a bowl and toss until well coated.

3 PLACE the coated chicken on the greased sheet pan and bake for about 35 minutes, or until cutting into the thickest piece reveals no pink.

4 SERVE garnished with a slice of lemon and a sprig of any one of the herbs used to make the rub.

POULTRY

MEATS

Tequila Marinated London Broil

Calories: 420 | Fat: 13g | Protein: 48g | Fiber: 0g | **Net Carbs: 2g**

When grilling steak, I tend to enter my "happy place," especially when it's marinated in tequila! Of course, the alcohol cooks out, leaving only a spicy, wonderful flavor behind, so the happiness comes from the tingling on my taste buds and not from the buzz of liquor!

MEATS

SHOPPING LIST

3 ½ pounds London broil

1 jalapeño pepper, seeded

1 clove garlic

1 cup tequila

1 cup teriyaki sauce

¼ cup sesame oil, optional

¼ cup Worcestershire sauce

¼ teaspoon kosher salt

¼ teaspoon black pepper

Cilantro leaves, for garnish

USING two forks, pierce the London broil repeatedly to tenderize the meat.

IN a blender, combine all remaining ingredients, except the garnish, processing until smooth.

PLACE London broil in a food storage bag or plastic container and pour marinade over top, turning it over to coat.

REFRIGERATE for at least 4 to 6 hours to marinate.

OIL and preheat a grill or grill-pan to high heat.

REMOVE London broil from marinade and place on the hot grill, cooking for 8 to 12 minutes (see next step).

WHILE cooking, flip the steak 4 times to create crisscrossing grill marks. Cooking time will vary with the thickness of the steak. (See hints for help determining the doneness of the steak.)

LET steak rest for 10 minutes under aluminum foil.

THINLY slice the steak against the grain of the meat and on a bias for wide, thin slices. Garnish with fresh cilantro, if desired.

HELPFUL HINTS

For medium rare steak, a meat thermometer inserted into the centermost part should read 130°F.

For medium - 145°F.

For medium well - 155°F.

For well done - 165°F.

MEATS

Citrus and Cilantro Pork Chops

Calories: 580 | Fat: 35g | Protein: 62g | Fiber: 0g | **Net Carbs: 0.5g**

Citrus and cilantro are the perfect pair for a quick and easy marinade like the one in this recipe. Once marinated, I sear the pork loin chops in a skillet to seal in all the flavors, though you could also grill them if you prefer.

SHOPPING LIST

2 pounds boneless pork loin chops, about ¾-inch thick

2 tablespoons olive oil

2 teaspoons orange zest

2 teaspoons lime juice

¼ cup fresh cilantro leaves, chopped

2 cloves garlic, crushed

½ teaspoon bulk sugar substitute (recommended: Splenda)

½ teaspoon kosher salt

⅛ teaspoon black pepper

HELPFUL HINTS

I also like to make these with tangerine zest for an even stronger citrus flavor.

1 PLACE pork chops in a large food storage container or baking dish.

2 WHISK together all remaining ingredients to create a marinade and pour over the pork, tossing all to coat well. Cover and refrigerate for 1 hour.

3 HEAT a large skillet or grill pan over medium-high heat until almost smoking hot.

4 SHAKE off any excess marinade and place pork chops in skillet and cook 5 to 6 minutes on each side, or until cutting into one reveals that it is mostly white throughout.

MEATS

Shepherd's Pie

Calories: 240 | Fat: 11.5g | Protein: 28g | Fiber: 2g | **Net Carbs: 2.5g**

As you may have noticed by now, cauliflower is one of my low carb staples! This magical chameleon vegetable absorbs flavors so well that you might even be fooled into thinking these were actual mashed potatoes, which are naturally the star of Shepherd's Pie—one of the most humbly delicious dishes I know of.

SHOPPING LIST

Vegetable oil spray

1 medium head cauliflower

1 pound ground beef

Salt and pepper

3 ounces cream cheese, softened

1 large egg

¼ cup grated Parmesan cheese

⅛ teaspoon chicken base or ½ teaspoon salt

⅛ teaspoon garlic powder

⅛ teaspoon black pepper

HELPFUL HINTS

Any ground meat can be used in this recipe. Ground lamb is actually traditional… not that cauliflower mashed potatoes are very traditional!

1 PREHEAT the oven to 375°F. Bring a pot of water to a boil over high heat, and then spray an 8x8-inch casserole dish with vegetable oil.

2 CLEAN and cut cauliflower into small pieces and place in the pot to boil for about 6 minutes until soft.

3 WHILE the cauliflower cooks, place the ground beef in a sauté pan over medium-high heat, add a dash of salt and pepper, and sauté until browned. Remove from heat, drain, and spread over the bottom of the casserole dish.

4 ONCE the cauliflower is cooked, drain well immediately and pat dry between layers of paper towels. Place the hot, dried cauliflower into a food processor along with the cream cheese, egg, Parmesan cheese, chicken base, garlic, and pepper, and blend until smooth.

5 SPOON the mashed cauliflower over top of the ground beef in the casserole dish, spreading to cover evenly. Bake for about 20 minutes, until the top starts to brown. Remove and let sit a few minutes before serving hot.

MEATS

Pork Souvlaki with Easy Tzatziki Sauce

Calories: 440 | Fat: 24g | Protein: 50g | Fiber: 0g | **Net Carbs: 3g**

Souvlaki was a dish introduced to me by a friend of mine that I had back in high school, whose mother had to be one of the best cooks I knew at the time. As it turns out, Pork Souvlaki is one of those afterschool meals that simply stuck with me. It is easily one of my favorite things to make for my own family, and the creamy, cucumber-infused flavor of the tzatziki sauce goes so perfectly that you'll be sure to find it unforgettable as well.

SHOPPING LIST

Eight 8-inch bamboo skewers

2 tablespoons extra virgin olive oil

2 tablespoons chopped fresh oregano leaves, plus 4 sprigs, for garnish

2 tablespoons minced red onion

1 ½ teaspoons kosher salt

1 teaspoon black pepper

2 garlic cloves, chopped

2 ½ pounds boneless pork loin, trimmed of all fat and cut into 1 ½-inch cubes

1 lemon, cut into wedges, for garnish

EASY TZATZIKI SAUCE

1 cup sour cream

½ cup minced cucumber, peeled and seeded

½ teaspoon minced fresh garlic

½ teaspoon kosher salt

HELPFUL HINTS

1 tablespoon of dried oregano can be used in place of the fresh oregano in a pinch.

1 SOAK bamboo skewers in water for 30 minutes to 1 hour (this will keep them from burning on the grill.)

2 IN a mixing bowl, whisk together the oil, oregano, onion, salt, pepper, and garlic to create a marinade.

3 TRANSFER the marinade to a plastic bag with the pork cubes and shake to coat well. Refrigerate for at least 30 minutes, or up to 12 hours.

4 MEANWHILE, add all Easy Tzatziki Sauce ingredients to a bowl and mix well. Cover and refrigerate until serving.

5 PREHEAT a grill or grill pan to high.

6 REMOVE the pork from the marinade and the skewers from the water, and thread 4 to 5 pieces of pork onto each skewer.

7 PLACE skewers on the edge of the grill, with the longest part of the stick hanging off, away from the fire. Stay close by and turn the sticks by hand to keep from burning. Skewers are done in just 4 to 5 minutes on each side.

8 SERVE each skewer accompanied by 1 tablespoon of Easy Tzatziki Sauce and garnish with sprigs of fresh oregano and lemon wedges, if desired.

BBQ Rub

Calories: 60 | Fat: 6g | Protein: 0g | Fiber: 1g | **Net Carbs: 1g**

All you have to do to make this quick rub for any backyard grilling day is check your pantry—chances are most of the ingredients are already there. The flavor, though, now that's some powerful Southern infusion!

SHOPPING LIST

¼ cup canola oil

2 tablespoons kosher salt

2 tablespoons paprika

1 ½ teaspoons black pepper

2 teaspoons garlic powder

2 teaspoons onion powder

1 PLACE all ingredients in a mixing bowl and stir with a fork until well combined.

2 KEEP covered and refrigerated in a plastic container for as long as 3 weeks.

HELPFUL HINTS

You can create a dry rub by simply leaving out the oil. The dry rub will keep for months on end.

MEATS

Bourbon BBQ Pork Ribs

Calories: 450 | Fat: 26g | Protein: 45g | Fiber: 1.5g | **Net Carbs: 4g**

These country-style pork ribs are extremely meaty and resemble beef short ribs but are less expensive than back ribs. The real key to success in cooking ribs of any kind, though, is in the sauce! Slow-cooking tenderizes meat until it begins to fall apart and the fat melts out, which infuses all those amazing barbecue flavors right into the meat. Of course, to add a little crispness, you'll definitely want to finish these on the grill!

SHOPPING LIST

4 to 5 pounds country-style pork ribs

Salt and black pepper

2 cups water

BOURBON BBQ SAUCE

1 (15-ounce) can tomato sauce

3 ounces tomato paste

1 ounce bourbon, may omit

1 tablespoon white vinegar

1 tablespoon liquid smoke

2 teaspoons Worcestershire sauce

¾ teaspoon hot sauce

½ cup bulk sugar substitute (recommended: Splenda)

2 tablespoons minced red onion

1 small garlic clove, minced

½ teaspoon onion powder

⅛ teaspoon garlic powder

1 ½ teaspoons kosher salt

½ teaspoon black pepper

1 Place the rack in the center of the oven and preheat the oven to 290°F.

2 Season the ribs generously with salt and pepper on both sides and then place in a deep roasting pan just large enough to fit the ribs in a single layer.

3 Whisk together all Bourbon BBQ Sauce ingredients until well combined.

4 Pour 1 cup barbecue sauce and 2 cups water over the ribs until they're almost completely submerged. If needed, add more sauce and water until covered or use a smaller pan.

5 Cover tightly with aluminum foil and bake for about 2 ½ hours until the meat is nearly falling off the bone.

6 Remove, drain the ribs immediately, and coat with the remaining ½ cup barbecue sauce.

7 Preheat a grill to high. Grill the ribs for just a few minutes on each side before serving.

MEATS

HELPFUL HINTS

If you find you don't plan on grilling immediately, refrigerate the precooked ribs and bring them back to room temperature whenever you're ready.

Chipotle Honey Glazed Ribs

Calories: 470 | Fat: 35g | Protein: 25.5g | Fiber: 1g | **Net Carbs: 7g**

The spice of chipotle and cayenne pepper in these slow cooked ribs is perfectly offset by the sweetness of honey. While I use only a small amount of real honey to keep the carb count low, you can use about ½ cup of honey and skip the sugar substitute, if desired.

SHOPPING LIST

3–4 pounds spareribs

2 tablespoons honey

½ cup bulk sugar substitute (recommended: Splenda)

⅓ cup white vinegar

1 cup tomato sauce

¼ cup tomato paste

2 tablespoons soy sauce

½ teaspoon dried thyme

½ teaspoon dried cilantro

½ teaspoon garlic powder

½ teaspoon chili powder

½ teaspoon ground cumin

¼ teaspoon crushed chipotle pepper, may use crushed red pepper

2 pinches of cayenne pepper

Toasted sesame seeds, for garnish

1 CUT spareribs into 3-rib sections to better fit into the slow cooker.

2 PLACE all remaining ingredients in cooker and stir to combine.

3 ADD the spareribs to the sauce in the cooker, set cooker to low, and cover.

4 COOK 8 to 10 hours, until the meat is tender and to your liking. (You can also cook these for 4 to 6 hours on high.)

5 SPRINKLE with toasted sesame seeds before serving, if desired.

HELPFUL HINTS

Try grilling the ribs or browning in a skillet before adding to the slow-cooker for even more flavor.

Steph's Chuck Pot Roast

Calories: 390 | Fat: 15g | Protein: 65g | Fiber: 0g | **Net Carbs: 1g**

This quick and easy pot roast is still my go-to recipe for the family classic. My big sister Stephanie's recipe, it's as close to my mother's preparation as either of us has ever been able to recreate. For a full meal, simply follow the preparation for Simply Roasted Vegetables (see page: 178) and add to the pot roast during the last 35 minutes of baking.

SHOPPING LIST

2 tablespoons canola oil

4 pounds boneless chuck roast

½ teaspoon kosher salt

½ teaspoon black pepper

¼ teaspoon garlic powder

½ teaspoon dried oregano

½ teaspoon dried basil

¼ teaspoon dried marjoram

2 large bay leaves

4 cups beef stock or broth

2 tablespoons tomato paste

1 PREHEAT the oven to 325°F.

2 ADD the oil to a large skillet or Dutch oven and place over medium-high heat until almost smoking hot.

3 SEASON the roast with the salt, pepper, and garlic powder, and place in the hot skillet.

4 SEAR on each side for 4 to 5 minutes until browned and then add the remaining ingredients.

5 COVER and bake for about 2 hours, until very tender and almost falling apart.

HELPFUL HINTS

Keep an eye on the roast as it bakes and add water if the cooking liquid cooks down below ½-inch. Any leftover au jus can be saved and frozen for use as beef stock for future dishes.

MEATS

Low Carb Beefed-Up Meatloaf

Calories: 355 | Fat: 15g | Protein: 46g | Fiber: 1.5g | **Net Carbs: 4.5g**

Who really needs breadcrumbs? Pounded out flat, layered with prosciutto and provolone cheese, and then rolled up and baked—this meatloaf may not be exactly what Mom used to make, but it's a sure-fire way to make someone happy!

SHOPPING LIST

1 (8-ounce) can tomato sauce

1 (6-ounce) can tomato paste

¼ cup bulk sugar substitute (recommended: Splenda)

2 teaspoons white vinegar

2 pounds ground chuck

2 large eggs

½ cup grated Parmesan cheese

¼ cup red onion, diced small

¼ cup roasted or fresh red bell peppers, diced

2 tablespoons chopped fresh parsley leaves

2 cloves garlic, minced

½ teaspoon dried oregano

½ teaspoon dried basil

1 teaspoon kosher salt

½ teaspoon black pepper

¼ pound prosciutto, or any type of ham, thinly sliced

¼ pound provolone cheese, sliced

HELPFUL HINTS

Prosciutto is usually available at the deli counter, but you must make sure to ask them to slice it extra thin or it will be too tough.

1 PREHEAT oven to 350°F.

2 IN a small bowl, combine the tomato sauce, tomato paste, sugar substitute, and vinegar. Set aside.

3 IN a large bowl, mix together the beef, eggs, Parmesan, vegetables, herbs, and seasonings.

4 WORKING on a waxed paper lined sheet pan or countertop, form the meatloaf mixture into a 10x8-inch flat rectangle on the waxed paper.

5 PLACE a layer of prosciutto slices on top of the meat, followed by a layer of provolone slices.

6 ROLL the stuffed meatloaf mixture up like a burrito and seal the edges all around by pinching the meat.

7 PLACE the roll, seam side down, into a 5x9-inch loaf pan. Spread a heavy coat of the tomato topping on top, completely covering the top of the meatloaf.

8 BAKE for about 1 hour and 15 minutes, or until the temperature on a meat thermometer registers 165°F. Drain fat and let rest at least 10 minutes before slicing.

MEATS

Grilled Herb Sirloin

Calories: 420 | Fat: 21g | Protein: 53g | Fiber: 0g | **Net Carbs: 0g**

Making this rub is a great way to use up any leftover fresh herbs. Since they are mixed with oil, these rubs can last 2 weeks in your fridge versus about 3 days for the fresh herbs alone. Sirloin steak is just one of the cuts of meat you can prepare this way, but it is definitely one I prepare often.

SHOPPING LIST

3 tablespoons olive oil

1 tablespoon fresh tarragon leaves, finely chopped

1 tablespoon chopped fresh parsley

1 tablespoon chopped fresh rosemary leaves

1 clove fresh garlic, minced

½ teaspoon kosher salt

¼ teaspoon black pepper

4 (8-ounce) boneless sirloin strip steaks

1 PREHEAT a grill or grill pan to high.

2 IN a mixing bowl, combine all of the ingredients, except the steaks, to create an herb rub.

3 RUB the steaks generously on all sides with the herb rub.

4 PLACE the steaks on the grill and cook 8 to 10 minutes for medium-rare, flipping halfway through. Serve garnished with sprigs of any of the fresh herbs.

HELPFUL HINTS

If you can't find fresh tarragon at your grocery store, you can substitute (easier to find) fresh basil.

MEATS

Grilled Ginger Pork Tenderloin

Calories: 340 | Fat: 16g | Protein: 44.5g | Fiber: 0g | **Net Carbs: 0g**

Pork tenderloin is not just one of the tenderest cuts of meat but also the leanest. In this recipe, I pair it with one of my favorite simple marinades of ginger and rosemary.

SHOPPING LIST

½ cup extra virgin olive oil

⅓ cup sherry vinegar or red wine vinegar

1 ½ tablespoons peeled, grated fresh ginger

1 tablespoon coarsely chopped fresh rosemary

1 clove fresh garlic, minced

½ teaspoon kosher salt

¼ teaspoon black pepper

¼ teaspoon crushed red pepper flakes, optional

2 (12-ounce) pork tenderloins, trimmed

HELPFUL HINTS

I also use this marinade for chicken, steaks, and seafood. In fact, this is an absolutely delicious combination with salmon.

1 IN a mixing bowl, whisk together oil, vinegar, ginger, garlic, rosemary, salt, pepper, and red pepper flakes to create a marinade.

2 TRANSFER ⅔ of the marinade to a large food storage bag or container and add the pork tenderloins. Refrigerate for at least 2 hours to marinate, refrigerating the remaining marinade separately.

3 BUILD a charcoal fire or preheat a gas grill or grill pan to high. Remove the pork from the bag and discard the used marinade.

4 PLACE the tenderloins on the grill and sear on all sides until cooked medium to medium rare, about 10 minutes, or when an instant-read thermometer stuck in the thickest piece reads 145°F.

5 TRANSFER the pork to a cutting board and let rest 5 minutes before cutting each into thin slices. Serve drizzled with the unused marinade and garnish with sprigs of fresh rosemary, if desired.

MEATS

Meat Lasagna

Calories: 350 | Fat: 19g | Protein: 40g | Fiber: 1g | **Net Carbs: 4g**

Honest ingredients such as the perfect amount of spices, a saucy meat filling, and plenty of melted cheeses are truly what a good lasagna is all about. Excluding the pasta seemed the natural thing to do, and I guarantee you won't even miss it!

SHOPPING LIST

2 tablespoons olive oil

2 cups diced celery

½ cup diced red onion

2 pounds ground beef

15 ounces tomato sauce (no sugar added)

1 teaspoon minced fresh garlic

1 teaspoon garlic powder

½ teaspoon salt

½ teaspoon black pepper

CHEESE FILLING

15 ounces ricotta cheese

4 cups shredded mozzarella cheese

½ cup grated Parmesan cheese

1 large egg

½ teaspoon minced fresh garlic

2 teaspoons dried Italian seasoning

1 teaspoon garlic powder

¼ teaspoon black pepper

1 PREHEAT the oven to 350°F. Heat the oil in a large skillet over medium-high heat. Add the celery and onion, and cook until slightly tender.

2 ADD the ground beef and cook until browned. Drain off the excess fat with a spoon or turkey baster.

3 ADD the tomato sauce, garlic, garlic powder, salt, and pepper, and simmer for 2 more minutes, stirring constantly. Remove from the heat.

4 MIX the ingredients for the cheese filling together in a bowl, using only half of the mozzarella.

5 FILL the bottom of a 13x9 baking dish with the meat filling and top with the cheese filling.

6 COVER the top with the remaining 8 ounces of mozzarella cheese.

7 BAKE for 45 to 50 minutes, until the top starts to become golden and bubbly.

8 LET cool for 10 minutes before slicing (the lasagna will hold together better).

HELPFUL HINTS

You can also make this with half ground beef and half crumbled Italian sausage for even more flavor.

MEATS

Mojo Pulled Pork

Calories: 465 | Fat: 23g | Protein: 60g | Fiber: 0g | **Net Carbs: 3g**

In Miami, Mojo Criollo roast pork is as common as Cuban coffee and can be found on street carts or classic outdoor walk-up luncheon counters. It's also the traditional way a spit-roasted pig is prepared, which, if I remember my chef days in South Florida, was served on just about every occasion!

SHOPPING LIST

1 boneless pork loin roast (about 4 pounds), trimmed

2 cups water

16 ounces Italian salad dressing

¼ cup fresh lime juice, about 2 limes

2 tablespoons chopped fresh cilantro leaves

2 small garlic cloves

1 teaspoon kosher salt

¼ teaspoon black pepper

1 ADD all the ingredients to a crock-pot and cook on high for 4 to 5 hours, or until the meat is easily flaked with a fork.

2 REMOVE cooked pork, reserving the liquid. Using two forks, pull apart and shred the meat.

3 SERVE hot, drizzled with some of the cooking liquid and garnished with fresh lime wedges and cilantro, if desired.

HELPFUL HINTS

Try making mini sandwiches using Zucchini Muffins (see page: 28) cut in half, griddled and topped with the pulled pork and melted Monterey jack cheese!

MEATS

Skillet Meat Pizza

Calories: 240 | Fat: 11g | Protein: 31g | Fiber: 0.5g | **Net Carbs: 3g**

Somewhere in between a pizza and a lasagna, I had a hard time coming up with a name for this one! This "Skillet Meat Pizza" is made meat-side down in a skillet and topped with spaghetti sauce and cheese. Skipping the crust gives you all the flavor with only 3 net carbs!

SHOPPING LIST

Vegetable oil spray

1 pound ground beef

1 large egg

¼ cup Parmesan cheese

1 teaspoon Italian seasoning

½ teaspoon garlic powder

½ teaspoon kosher salt

¼ teaspoon black pepper

1 cup pizza or spaghetti sauce, no-sugar added variety

1 cup shredded mozzarella cheese

HELPFUL HINTS

Feel free to top this pie with your favorite pizza toppings—anything from pepperoni and sausage to sliced bell peppers, mushrooms, or onions works perfectly!

1 PREHEAT the oven to 375°F and spray the skillet with vegetable oil.

2 IN a large bowl, mix together the beef, egg, Parmesan cheese, and seasonings.

3 PLACE the meat mixture into the skillet and press down to spread evenly over the entire bottom of the pan and slightly up the sides. Bake for about 12 minutes, just until cooked. Remove from the oven and drain any excess grease.

4 SPREAD the pizza sauce evenly over the cooked and drained meat crust and sprinkle the mozzarella cheese over all.

5 RETURN the skillet to the oven and bake for an additional 8 to 10 minutes until the cheese melts and starts to brown. Remove and cut into 6 pieces to serve.

MEATS

Prep Time	Cook Time	Serves
10 min	30 min	6

Simple Seared London Broil

Calories: 360 | Fat: 14.5g | Protein: 52g | Fiber: 0g | **Net Carbs: 0g**

Steak in an oven can be horrible, but the trick is searing it first to seal in the juices! This is actually how we cook many meats in restaurant kitchens—we keep our ovens at 550 degrees for just such "searing and baking" of anything from thick cut steaks and chops to racks of lamb—they all get pan seared and then popped in the oven to finish.

SHOPPING LIST

2 tablespoons canola oil

3 pound average London broil steak, shoulder London broil is what we use

½ teaspoon kosher salt

¼ teaspoon black pepper

⅛ teaspoon garlic powder

HELPFUL HINTS

Watch the cooking time, as the thinner the steak, the less time it will take to cook at 400°F. Of course it may also take longer if the steak is thick.

1 PREHEAT the oven to 400°F.

2 HEAT the oil in a large skillet over medium-high heat until almost smoking hot.

3 SEASON the steak evenly on both sides with the salt, pepper, and garlic powder, and add to the hot pan.

4 SEAR on each side for about 2 to 3 minutes, until browned.

5 ADD seared London broil to a shallow roasting pan and bake for about 15 minutes or until a meat thermometer inserted in the thickest part reads 145°F for medium-rare.

6 LET steak rest for 5 minutes before cutting thin slices against the grain of the meat and serve immediately.

MEATS

SEAFOOD

Prep Time 20 min	Cook Time 6 min	Serves 4

Anaheim Shrimp Scampi

Calories: 365 | Fat: 25g | Protein: 28.5g | Fiber: 2.5g | **Net Carbs: 4g**

For nearly three decades now, I have been preparing this recipe for a California-inspired take on shrimp scampi that features Asiago cheese and avocado. Though I usually say, "Don't go without, reinvent," that proclamation hardly even applies here, as this was always naturally low in carbs. While I used to serve it over pasta before my weight loss, I've now been enjoying it over low carb spaghetti squash (and not missing a thing!) for more than 10 years.

SHOPPING LIST

6 tablespoons Scampi Butter (see page: 146)

1 small spaghetti squash

1 pound (16 to 20 count) peeled and deveined raw shrimp, with tail on

1 tablespoon dry white wine

2 ounces crumbled Asiago cheese

1 avocado, peeled and chopped

Fresh arugula leaves, for garnish

HELPFUL HINTS

Nutritional information for this recipe was calculated using Scampi Butter made from real butter. Using light, trans-fat free buttery spread to prepare the Scampi Butter will reduce the calories in this recipe to 295 and the fat to 17 grams.

PREPARE the Scampi Butter according to the recipe's directions.

CUT the squash in half lengthwise and scoop out all seeds.

BRING a large pot of water to a boil. Completely submerge the squash halves in the boiling water and cook for 20 to 25 minutes, until a fork can easily pull the squash into strands.

DRAIN and run cold water over the squash to stop the cooking process.

USE a fork to scrape the cooked squash out of its rind, fluffing and separating the pulp into spaghetti-like strands.

PLACE 4 tablespoons of the Scampi Butter in a large sauté pan over high heat until melted.

ADD the shrimp and cook for about 2 minutes, stirring occasionally.

ADD the white wine, which will sizzle in the pan, and cook until the shrimp are opaque, about another 2 minutes.

MICROWAVE the strands of spaghetti squash for 30 seconds, just until reheated.

REMOVE shrimp from heat and stir in the remaining 2 tablespoons Scampi Butter, the Asiago cheese, and avocado.

SERVE over the hot spaghetti squash, garnished with fresh arugula.

Scampi Butter

Calories: 70 | Fat: 7.5g | Protein: 0g | Fiber: 0g | **Net Carbs: 0g**

This "compound" butter is a staple that you can make in advance and melt over seafood, any cut of meat, or even stir into vegetables to add a full recipe's worth of flavor all at once. Nutritional information is for a serving of 1 tablespoon prepared with real butter. Using the suggested buttery spread will reduce the calories to 35 and fat to 3.5 grams per serving. Makes 12 tablespoons.

SHOPPING LIST

½ cup (1 stick) unsalted butter, softened (may use light, trans-fat free buttery spread)

Juice of 1 lemon

1 tablespoon minced fresh garlic

2 tablespoons minced red onion

1 tablespoon chopped fresh parsley

½ teaspoon garlic powder

1 tablespoon kosher salt

¼ teaspoon black pepper

Dash of ground white pepper

Dash of Worcestershire sauce

1 IN a bowl, whisk together all ingredients until well blended. It takes a bit of work at first, but if you keep whisking, it will mix together.

2 SPOON the compound butter onto a piece of plastic wrap and form it into a log about 2 inches around. Roll the plastic wrap up into a cylinder and twist the ends shut.

3 YOU may store the butter in the refrigerator for 1 week or freeze for as long as 1 year.

HELPFUL HINTS

If you have trouble combining the ingredients, the butter is most likely not soft enough. Microwave for just a few seconds at a time until the butter is soft enough to work with.

SEAFOOD

Shrimp and Scallion Stir Fry

Calories: 205 | Fat: 10.5g | Protein: 25g | Fiber: 1g | **Net Carbs: 1.5g**

I love a simple stir fry and it doesn't get much more simple than this! The slightly sweet shrimp are wonderfully offset by the spice of scallions and fresh garlic—but don't worry—most of the heat of the onions cooks out.

SHOPPING LIST

2 tablespoons canola oil

2 teaspoons sesame oil

1 pound medium-sized peeled and deveined shrimp

1 small bunch scallions, ends trimmed and sliced into 1-inch lengths

1 clove garlic, crushed

2 tablespoons soy sauce

¼ teaspoon black pepper

Toasted sesame seeds, optional

HELPFUL HINTS

You can (and should) add in any veggies you may have in your fridge for a heartier meal.

1 POUR the canola oil and sesame oil in a sauté pan or wok over medium-high heat and bring up to a sizzle.

2 ADD the shrimp and cook, stirring constantly, for about 4 minutes.

3 ADD the scallions, garlic, soy sauce, and black pepper, and sauté an additional 2 minutes.

4 REMOVE from heat and serve immediately, garnished with toasted sesame seeds, if desired.

SEAFOOD

Shrimp Mousse Stuffed Tilapia

Calories: 440 | Fat: 31g | Protein: 36g | Fiber: 0g | **Net Carbs: 3g**

As a chef in the mid-eighties, I was given a new breed of freshwater, farm-raised fish to experiment with after I helped promote aquaculture farming with the Florida Department of Natural Resources and Seafood Marketing Bureau. As it turns out, this new breed's mild flavor caught on in Florida and throughout restaurants in the rest of the country, making tilapia one of the most popular fish today. Here, it's the perfect entertaining roulade, stuffed with the fresh, complementary flavors of shrimp, white wine, and lemon.

SHOPPING LIST

2 tablespoons unsalted butter

1 pound peeled and deveined raw shrimp, any size

1 cup heavy cream

¼ teaspoon kosher salt

⅛ teaspoon black pepper

⅛ teaspoon ground nutmeg

1 tablespoon diced roasted red pepper

1 tablespoon chopped fresh parsley

4 medium tilapia fillets, cut in half down the center to make 8 long pieces

2 tablespoons fresh lemon juice

2 ounces dry white wine

Kosher salt and black pepper

4 sprigs fresh basil, for garnish

Lemon wedges, for garnish

HELPFUL HINTS

If you are unsure if the mousse has cooked all the way through, simply stick a toothpick down the center of it and see if it comes out clean.

1 PREHEAT the oven to 375°F. Coat a sheet pan generously with butter.

2 DICE one-quarter of the peeled raw shrimp and reserve. Place the remaining shrimp, cream, ¼ teaspoon salt, ⅛ teaspoon pepper, and nutmeg in a food processor and blend on high for about 30 seconds until thick and creamy. Transfer to a bowl and mix in the reserved diced shrimp, red pepper, and parsley.

3 WORKING over the sheet pan, place a heaping tablespoon of the mousse on each tilapia fillet half, quickly wrap the fillet in a circle around the mousse, and place upright close together on the sheet pan. (The mousse should hold the tilapia fillet in place like glue.)

4 DRIZZLE the roulades with lemon juice and wine and season lightly with salt and pepper.

5 BAKE for about 10 minutes, just until the mousse in the center rises and browns. Serve 2 roulades per plate, garnished with fresh basil sprigs and 2 wedges of lemon, if desired.

SEAFOOD

Tilapia with Bacon and Artichokes

Calories: 220 | Fat: 8g | Protein: 31g | Fiber: 4g | **Net Carbs: 3g**

Tilapia is just one of those fish with a light, neutral flavor that just about anyone can appreciate with the right ingredients! Bacon, marinated artichoke hearts, and roasted red peppers bring an aromatic, zesty finish to this very healthy dish!

SHOPPING LIST

4 slices thick-cut bacon, chopped

4 tilapia fillets

Kosher salt and black pepper

1 (10-ounce) jar marinated artichoke hearts, drained and quartered

2 tablespoons diced roasted red peppers

Juice of ½ a lemon

1 tablespoon chopped flat-leaf parsley

HELPFUL HINTS

Diced pancetta (Italian bacon) is even better than bacon in this recipe; though it can be a tough (and expensive) ingredient to find.

1 PLACE bacon in a large pan over medium-high heat and cook until crisp. Remove from pan and set aside, leaving bacon grease in the pan.

2 REDUCE heat to medium, generously season tilapia fillets with salt and pepper, and place in pan. Let fillets sear for 3 minutes without moving them.

3 FLIP fillets and cook an additional minute before adding the cooked bacon, artichoke hearts, roasted red peppers, and lemon juice. Let cook until artichokes are warmed and fish easily flakes with a fork, 1 to 2 minutes.

4 SPRINKLE with parsley before serving.

SEAFOOD

Crushed Walnut Tilapia

Calories: 380 | Fat: 24g | Protein: 36g | Fiber: 1g | **Net Carbs: 3g**

You just can't have enough tilapia; it's inexpensive as far as seafood goes, readily available almost anywhere these days, and has a very mild taste that almost everyone enjoys. Topping tilapia with crushed walnuts adds not only great flavor, but a nice crunch to offset the flaky fish.

SHOPPING LIST

Vegetable oil spray

2 tilapia fillets (filet of sole or flounder may be used)

1 ounce white wine, optional, may use water

2 teaspoons fresh lemon juice

1 tablespoon mayonnaise

2 tablespoons softened butter

1 teaspoon Dijon mustard

¼ teaspoon kosher salt

⅛ teaspoon black pepper

¼ cup crushed or finely chopped walnuts

1 PREHEAT the oven to 375°F and coat a baking dish with vegetable oil.

2 PLACE the tilapia filets in the baking dish and drizzle with the wine and lemon juice.

3 ADD all remaining ingredients, except the walnuts, to a medium bowl and mix well to create a glaze.

4 TOP the fish with even amounts of the glaze and then sprinkle with the crushed walnuts.

5 BAKE for 15 minutes, or until the fish starts to brown and easily flakes with a fork. Serve basted in the pan juices and garnished with lemon wedges, if desired.

HELPFUL HINTS

Tilapia fillets cut in half perfectly (as they are already segmented down the middle). Make a double batch of this recipe and cut each fillet in half for 8 appetizer-sized portions.

SEAFOOD

Blackening Spice

Calories: 5 | Fat: 0g | Protein: 0g | Fiber: 0g | **Net Carbs: 0g**

Store-bought seasonings are oftentimes full of unnecessary fillers and sugars. This spice mixture is so chock-full of flavor, and since all you have to do is throw everything into a bowl and shake together, you'll most certainly find yourself using it all the time! With it, I've been making the most excellent blackened chicken, pork chops, and seafood for decades now. Literally, it has been a family staple since the early 80's.

SHOPPING LIST

5 tablespoons kosher salt

5 tablespoons paprika

1 tablespoon dried thyme

1 tablespoon black pepper

1 tablespoon garlic powder

½ teaspoon cayenne pepper

½ teaspoon ground white pepper

1 MIX all ingredients together.

2 STORE in an airtight container or empty spice canister.

HELPFUL HINTS

Since this recipe makes about 1 cup, you can always double or triple it and keep plenty around for easy access during a busy workweek. It's great for grilling, baking, or pan-frying anything, from poultry to your favorite vegetables.

SEAFOOD

Shrimp Mock Fried Rice

Calories: 180 | Fat: 11g | Protein: 16g | Fiber: 1.5g | **Net Carbs: 3g**

When we began our low carb lifestyle, we were not about to just give up on one of our favorite cuisines—who doesn't like Chinese food, anyway? We came up with this recipe for exactly that reason by using grated cauliflower in place of the rice and keeping all those awesome flavors intact!

SHOPPING LIST

2 cups raw cauliflower

2 tablespoons vegetable oil

2 tablespoons finely diced red bell pepper

4 tablespoons thinly sliced scallions

½ cup cooked salad shrimp

¼ teaspoon minced fresh garlic

3 tablespoons soy sauce

3 large eggs, beaten

Salt to taste, if needed.

HELPFUL HINTS

It's completely normal for there to be extra liquid in the pan when this is finished. Use a slotted spoon to drain it as you serve.

1 GRATE the fresh cauliflower using the largest holes of a cheese grater. You can also use a food processor fitted with a grating blade.

2 HEAT the oil in a large skillet over medium-high heat. Add the bell pepper and 3 tablespoons of the green onions, and cook for 1 minute.

3 ADD the cauliflower, shrimp, and garlic and cook, stirring constantly, for 4 to 5 minutes until the cauliflower is tender.

4 ADD the soy sauce and stir. Add the eggs to one corner of the pan but don't stir for 1 minute. This allows the eggs to cook for a bit, which will prevent them from completely breaking up and disappearing into the mix.

5 As soon as the eggs are soft-cooked, remove the skillet from the heat and gently fold the eggs into the mixture. Add salt or more soy sauce to taste and serve garnished with the remaining 1 tablespoon of green onions.

SEAFOOD

Baked Parmesan Shrimp

Calories: 325 | Fat: 19g | Protein: 35g | Fiber: 0g | **Net Carbs: 0.5g**

These shrimp are truly supreme. Topped with a creamy Parmesan cheese topping that browns as it bakes, you'll be surprised by how something so simple can be so delicious!

SHOPPING LIST

Vegetable oil spray

1 pound large peeled and deveined shrimp, tail-on

2 teaspoons fresh lemon juice

¼ cup Parmesan cheese

2 tablespoons mayonnaise

2 tablespoons butter, softened

1 teaspoon chopped fresh parsley

¼ teaspoon kosher salt

¼ teaspoon Italian seasoning

⅛ teaspoon black pepper

1 PREHEAT the oven to 375°F and spray a 2-quart baking dish with vegetable oil spray.

2 PLACE the shrimp in the baking dish and drizzle with the lemon juice.

3 COMBINE all remaining ingredients and evenly top the shrimp with the mixture.

4 BAKE for 12 to 15 minutes, or until the coated shrimp start to brown. Serve garnished with lemon wedges, if desired.

HELPFUL HINTS

For best browning results, coat each shrimp evenly by holding a shrimp in one hand while you spread the Parmesan-mixture on it with the other, and then place mixture-side up in the baking dish.

SEAFOOD

Spaghetti Squash Crab Alfredo

Calories: 310 | Fat: 23g | Protein: 20g | Fiber: 0g | **Net Carbs: 5g**

Crab and Alfredo is a truly perfect pair that makes for an absolutely decadent sauce for low carb spaghetti squash. Sprinkling with a garnish of Old Bay seasoning is an absolute must!

SHOPPING LIST

1 spaghetti squash

4 tablespoons unsalted butter

1 cup heavy cream

1 clove garlic, crushed

1 ½ cups freshly grated Parmesan cheese

¼ cup chopped fresh parsley leaves

8 ounces claw crabmeat

2 tablespoons finely diced red bell pepper

Old Bay seasoning

HELPFUL HINTS

The crabmeat used in this recipe can be found in cans or refrigerated tubs in your grocer's seafood department. Jumbo lump crabmeat is even better than the claw meat but nearly three times the price!

1 CUT the squash in half lengthwise and scoop out all seeds.

2 BRING a large pot of water to a boil. Completely submerge the squash halves in the boiling water and cook for 20 to 25 minutes, until a fork can easily pull the squash into strands.

3 DRAIN and run cold water over the squash to stop the cooking process.

4 USE a fork to scrape the cooked squash out of its rind, fluffing and separating the pulp into spaghetti-like strands.

5 MELT 2 tablespoons of the butter in a sauce pot over medium-high heat. Add the cream to the sauce pot and let simmer 2 minutes to reduce.

6 WHISK garlic and cheese into the sauce until combined. Remove from heat and fold in parsley, crabmeat, and remaining butter.

7 MICROWAVE the strands of spaghetti squash for 30 to 45 seconds to reheat.

8 TOP the warm spaghetti squash strands with the hot sauce from the stove and serve garnished with diced bell pepper and a generous sprinkling of Old Bay seasoning.

SEAFOOD

Roasted Pecan and Herb-Crusted Salmon

Calories: 465 | Fat: 30.5g | Protein: 51g | Fiber: 2.5g | **Net Carbs: 4g**

My Roasted Pecan and Herb-Crusted Salmon is an absolute signature recipe for me. In fact, I even have a signature dish I must prepare it in. Handed down to me from my mother, you can see the decades-old steel baking dish at left!

SHOPPING LIST

1 small fennel bulb, cored and thinly sliced

2 plum tomatoes, halved

1 cup julienned bell peppers (any color)

½ cup sliced red onion

2 tablespoons extra virgin olive oil

½ teaspoon kosher salt

⅛ teaspoon garlic powder

⅛ teaspoon black pepper

SALMON

2 tablespoons chopped fennel fronds

2 tablespoons chopped fresh basil

1 ½ tablespoons Dijon mustard

½ teaspoon kosher salt

⅛ teaspoon black pepper

2 pounds boneless, skinless salmon fillets

2 ounces dry white wine

2 tablespoons fresh lemon juice

2 tablespoons butter, melted

½ cup chopped pecans

1 PREHEAT the oven to 400°F. Combine all of the first set of ingredients in a shallow roasting pan and toss to mix. Spread the mixture out to form a bed for the salmon.

2 IN a small bowl, mix the fennel fronds, basil, mustard, salt, and pepper. Rub each salmon fillet with the mixture and arrange the fillets over the top of the vegetable bed.

3 DRIZZLE all with the wine and lemon juice.

4 COMBINE the melted butter and pecans in a small bowl and top each fillet with it.

5 BAKE until salmon is just cooked through and the vegetables are tender, 15 to 17 minutes. Serve each piece of salmon atop vegetables, just as it was baked. Garnish with lemon wedges, if desired.

HELPFUL HINTS

Though you can use any dry white wine, I always prepare this with vermouth.

SEAFOOD

Slow Cooker Jambalaya

Calories: 190 | Fat: 8.5g | Protein: 19.5g | Fiber: 2.5g | **Net Carbs: 6g**

Jambalaya was always a favorite of mine—probably because I'd eat a big bowl of seafood any day and in any way! In this simple slow cooker version, I've replaced the traditional rice with grated cauliflower to cut out most of the carbs it would normally contain.

SHOPPING LIST

2 cups chopped cooked kielbasa sausage, may use any cooked sausage

1 cup chopped celery

1 cup chopped green bell pepper

1 cup chopped white or yellow onion

1 (28-ounce) can diced tomatoes, with juice

2 cloves minced garlic

½ teaspoon Tobasco hot sauce

1 tablespoon cumin

½ teaspoon kosher salt

¼ teaspoon black pepper

1 pound medium-sized peeled and deveined shrimp

2 cups raw cauliflower

1 PLACE all of the ingredients, except the shrimp, and cauliflower into a slow cooker set to low and stir to combine.

2 COOK on low for 4 to 6 hours (depending on when you are ready to eat).

3 USING the large holes of a cheese grater, grate the raw cauliflower into small, rice-like pieces.

4 ADD the shrimp and cauliflower to the cooker and cook for just another 20 to 30 minutes before serving.

HELPFUL HINTS

Jambalaya is traditionally made with Andouille sausage instead of kielbasa, but that may be hard to find in your local grocery store.

SEAFOOD

VEGETABLES AND SIDES

Cauliflower Rice Pilaf

Calories: 100 | Fat: 8.5g | Protein: 2.5g | Fiber: 2g | **Net Carbs: 2g**

Rice Pilaf, featuring freshly grated cauliflower, has been one of our go-to sidekicks for years now since we have a tendency to crave things familiar to us. Of course it can be one your favorites now too - seeing as how I'm sharing it with you!

SHOPPING LIST

¼ cup slivered almonds

1 small head cauliflower

1 tablespoon unsalted butter

1 tablespoon olive oil

2 tablespoons chopped yellow onion

¼ teaspoon minced fresh garlic

1 cup chicken broth

1 teaspoon chopped fresh parsley

2 bay leaves

½ teaspoon turmeric

½ teaspoon kosher salt

¼ teaspoon black pepper

PLACE the slivered almonds in a large skillet over medium heat to toast.

SHAKE the pan every 30 seconds or so to redistribute, cooking just until they are golden brown and smell fragrant, about 4 to 5 minutes. Remove almonds from pan and set aside.

USING the largest holes of a cheese grater, grate the head of cauliflower (as you would cheese). A food processor with a grating blade will also work.

SIDES

Heat the butter and oil in a large skillet over medium-high heat.

Add the chicken broth and all remaining ingredients, and simmer for about 9 minutes, stirring occasionally, until cauliflower is tender.

Add the onion, garlic, and grated cauliflower to the skillet and sauté for 2 minutes, stirring constantly.

Stir in toasted almonds and serve with a slotted spoon.

HELPFUL HINTS

It's completely normal for there to be extra liquid in the pan when this is finished. Use a slotted spoon to drain it as you serve.

Charred Green Beans

Calories: 95 | Fat: 7g | Protein: 2g | Fiber: 4g | **Net Carbs: 4g**

We chefs cook almost everything at 500 degrees—not only because we have to get a 30 minute dish out in 15 minutes—but also because it seals in the goodness and brings out natural sugars and flavors as the food browns. This is definitely the case with these "charred" green beans. When you think they're burning, trust me, they are only getting better!

SHOPPING LIST

1 pound fresh green beans, ends trimmed

2 tablespoons olive oil

1 teaspoon Blackening Spice (see page: 153)

Diced pimentos, for garnish

HELPFUL HINTS

It's a good idea to make sure that your oven is clean and free from crumbs before cooking at such a high temperature as it may smoke otherwise.

1 PREHEAT the oven to 525°F.

2 PLACE all ingredients in a very heavy roasting pan or sizzler platter and toss to coat.

3 BAKE for 8 to 12 minutes, until the green beans appear charred. Serve immediately, garnished with a sprinkling of diced pimentos, if desired.

SIDES

Spaghetti Squash with Ricotta and Ham

Calories: 155 | Fat: 7g | Protein: 13g | Fiber: 0g | **Net Carbs: 5g**

This Italian "pasta" dish is topped with an Alfredo-like sauce made from ricotta cheese, so it stays thick and creamy without the need of starchy thickeners. The ham is meant to add flavor to this side dish, but you can also add additional ham and broccoli or spinach to make this into a complete entrée.

SHOPPING LIST

1 medium spaghetti squash

1 ½ cups ricotta cheese

½ cup chicken broth, may use vegetable broth

½ cup diced baked ham

¼ cup diced roasted red peppers, may use tomatoes

1 teaspoon minced garlic

½ teaspoon dried oregano

2 teaspoons chopped fresh basil leaves

¼ cup grated Parmesan cheese

Kosher salt and black pepper

HELPFUL HINTS

This is also really great with sliced prosciutto or cooked bacon in place of the ham.

1 CUT the squash in half lengthwise and scoop out all seeds.

2 BRING a large pot of water to a boil. Completely submerge the squash halves in the boiling water and cook for 20 to 25 minutes, until a fork can easily pull the squash into strands.

3 As the squash is cooking, place a sauce pot over medium heat and add the ricotta cheese, chicken broth, ham, garlic, oregano, and basil. Bring to a slow simmer, stirring continuously. Add the Parmesan cheese and then salt and pepper to taste. Turn heat to low and keep warm until serving, stirring occasionally.

4 DRAIN and run cold water over the squash to stop the cooking process.

5 USE a fork to scrape the cooked squash out of its rind, fluffing and separating the pulp into spaghetti-like strands. Microwave for 30 seconds to reheat.

6 TOP the warm spaghetti squash strands with the hot sauce from the stove and serve garnished with fresh basil leaves or parsley, if desired.

SIDES

Loaded Baked Cauliflower

Calories: 245 | Fat: 19g | Protein: 13g | Fiber: 2g | **Net Carbs: 3.5g**

While I am starting to wonder exactly how many times I can reinvent the classic potato skin appetizer, these baked cauliflower florets topped with cheese, bacon, and sour cream are my favorite low carb version yet! Who needs that starchy potato shell when you can enjoy all the good stuff on top without it?

SHOPPING LIST

Vegetable oil spray

1 medium head cauliflower, cored and coarsely chopped

2 tablespoons olive oil

1 teaspoon kosher salt

¼ teaspoon black pepper

¼ teaspoon garlic powder

¾ cup shredded Cheddar cheese

6 strips bacon, cooked and coarsely chopped

⅓ cup sour cream

1 scallion, thinly sliced

HELPFUL HINTS

If you are watching both your carbs and fat intake, low-fat versions of the cheese and sour cream can be used in place of the regular versions used here. The bacon can be replaced with turkey bacon or omitted entirely, if desired.

1 PREHEAT the oven to 425°F and spray a sheet pan with vegetable oil.

2 IN a large bowl, combine cauliflower, olive oil, salt, pepper, and garlic powder and mix well to coat.

3 TRANSFER the seasoned cauliflower to a sheet pan, spreading them out in a single layer.

4 BAKE for about 15 minutes, until just tender, and remove from oven.

5 TOP the cooked cauliflower evenly with the Cheddar cheese and cooked bacon pieces and return to the oven for another 5 minutes, just until cheese is melted and bubbly. Serve hot, garnished with a dollop of sour cream and sliced scallions.

SIDES

Sweet Potato Casserole

Calories: 165 | Fat: 8g | Protein: 5g | Fiber: 3.5g | **Net Carbs: 16g**

This Sweet Potato Casserole based on an older (and too darn difficult) recipe for stuffed sweet potatoes was created this last Thanksgiving—but here's the weird part—our friend and community member, Dinah Moore, was making the exact same thing at the exact same time! So I thought I'd give her a little coincidental credit!

SHOPPING LIST

Vegetable oil spray

6 large sweet potatoes, cooked (see hints)

3 large egg yolks

2 tablespoons heavy cream

⅓ cup bulk sugar substitute (recommended: Splenda)

1 ½ teaspoons vanilla extract

1 teaspoon pumpkin pie spice

½ cup chopped pecans

MERINGUE

3 large egg whites

½ teaspoon vanilla extract

¼ teaspoon cream of tartar

¼ cup bulk sugar substitute (recommended: Splenda)

1 PREHEAT oven to 325°F. Spray a 2 quart baking dish with vegetable oil spray.

2 SLICE baked sweet potatoes in half and scoop all cooked pulp into a large mixing bowl. Discard skins.

3 WHISK egg yolks, heavy cream, sugar substitute, vanilla extract, and pumpkin pie spice into the sweet potatoes until well combined.

4 BEAT all Meringue ingredients in an electric mixer on high for 2 to 3 minutes, until soft peaks can be made.

5 FOLD the chopped pecans and ⅓ of the Meringue into the sweet potato mixture and spread across the bottom of the prepared baking dish.

6 TOP the sweet potato mixture with the remaining Meringue and bake 35 to 40 minutes, just until the topping is golden brown.

HELPFUL HINTS

The sweet potatoes can be pierced with a fork several times and microwaved 5 to 8 minutes to cook, just until soft.

SIDES

Cranberry Relish

Calories: 20 | Fat: 0g | Protein: 0g | Fiber: 1g | **Net Carbs: 3g**

It wouldn't be the holidays without cranberries, so we're quite lucky they're naturally low in sugar. Of course, the kinds of sauces you'll find premade in supermarkets are full of the stuff. Which is why this relish is so darn delicious—because it's made fresh, and isn't it all about the cranberries anyway?

SHOPPING LIST

1 cup bulk sugar substitute (recommended: Splenda)

1 cup water

12 ounces cranberries, fresh or frozen

1 teaspoon freshly grated orange zest

HELPFUL HINTS

Be sure to rinse the cranberries well, removing any stems or rotten berries before cooking.

1 COMBINE the sugar substitute and water in a saucepan and bring to a boil on the stove.

2 ADD the cranberries and orange zest, and bring back to a boil. Reduce the heat to low and simmer for 10 minutes, stirring occasionally.

3 REMOVE from the heat and let cool before covering and placing in the refrigerator until ready to serve.

Zucchini Parmesan Sauté

Calories: 60 | Fat: 4g | Protein: 2g | Fiber: 1g | **Net Carbs: 2.5g**

If you're anything like us, you need an extensive arsenal of quick and easy sides to round out an easy family meal. I've seen many a vegetable or side dish that was 10 times as complicated as the grilled steak or chicken it accompanied. That doesn't make much sense to me! The entire meal should be easy-smeazy and, of course, cheesy! And just like the story goes, this zucchini sauté has it all!

SHOPPING LIST

1 tablespoon olive oil

¼ cup sliced red onion

2 medium zucchini, cut into ¼ inch-thick slices on the diagonal

1 small clove garlic, minced

½ teaspoon kosher salt

½ teaspoon Italian seasoning

⅛ teaspoon black pepper

2 tablespoons grated Parmesan cheese

1 HEAT the oil in a large skillet over medium-high heat.

2 ADD all of the ingredients, except the Parmesan cheese, and cook, stirring occasionally, until lightly browned and crisp-tender, about 2 minutes.

3 REMOVE from heat, sprinkle with the Parmesan cheese, and serve hot, garnished with diced pimento or tomatoes, if desired.

HELPFUL HINTS

Try adding any combination of cubed eggplant, artichoke hearts, yellow squash, mushrooms, or even asparagus spears to make this a "kitchen sink" recipe that's different, depending on what's in your refrigerator!

SIDES

Original Cauliflower Mac and Cheese Casserole

Calories: 190 | Fat: 15g | Protein: 7g | Fiber: 3g | **Net Carbs: 4g**

When I first came up with this recipe as a way to appease Christian's love for Macaroni and Cheese, I had no idea it would go on to become one of my most popular recipes of all time. In fact, it's the 4th highest rated cauliflower recipe (out of over 300) on Food Network's website. Oh, and by the way, the number 1 cauliflower recipe on their site is also in this book... my Mock Mashed Potatoes (see page: 179).

SHOPPING LIST

Kosher salt, as needed, plus ½ teaspoon

Vegetable oil spray

1 large head cauliflower, cut into small florets

¾ cup heavy cream

2 ounces cream cheese, cut into small pieces

1 ½ teaspoons Dijon mustard

1 ½ cups shredded sharp Cheddar cheese, plus ½ cup for topping the casserole

¼ teaspoon black pepper

⅛ teaspoon garlic powder

HELPFUL HINTS

To save on paper towels, we've found that you can place the cauliflower in a colander and drain the excess water by pressing down on the florets with a heavy bowl.

1 PREHEAT the oven to 375°F. Bring a large pot of water to a boil, seasoning the water with salt. Spray an 8x8 baking dish with vegetable oil spray.

2 COOK the cut cauliflower in the boiling water until crisp-tender, about 5 minutes.

3 DRAIN well and pat between several layers of paper towels to dry. Transfer the cauliflower to the baking dish and set aside.

4 BRING the cream to a simmer in a small sauce-pan and then whisk in the cream cheese and mustard, continuously whisking until smooth.

5 STIR in the 1 ½ cups of cheese, salt, pepper, and garlic powder, and whisk just until the cheese melts, about 2 minutes. Remove the sauce from the heat, pour over the cauliflower, and stir all to combine.

6 TOP with the remaining ½ cup cheese and bake until browned and bubbly hot, about 15 to 20 minutes. Let cool 5 minutes before serving.

SIDES

Simply Roasted Vegetables

Calories: 90 | Fat: 4.5g | Protein: 3g | Fiber: 3g | **Net Carbs: 7g**

There's just something about a colorful dish that draws you in. Of course, we eat with our eyes first, don't we? Well, there's a reason for that, and I've been using it as my motto for years—when you're cooking with color, you're cooking healthy!

SHOPPING LIST

Vegetable oil spray

3 stalks celery, cut into thirds

2 medium yellow squash, halved crosswise

2 medium zucchini, halved crosswise

1 medium yellow onion, quartered

1 red bell pepper, cored, seeded, and quartered

1 clove garlic, minced

2 tablespoons olive oil

1 ½ teaspoons kosher salt

1 teaspoon dried oregano

1 teaspoon paprika

¼ teaspoon black pepper

⅛ teaspoon garlic powder

1 PREHEAT the oven to 350°F and spray a roasting pan with vegetable oil.

2 IN a large bowl, toss together vegetables with all remaining ingredients.

3 ARRANGE the vegetables in the roasting pan and bake for 35 to 40 minutes, until well done. Serve hot.

HELPFUL HINTS

These vegetables can be baked right alongside or underneath many of the entrée dishes in this book. Any cut of meat that bakes at 325°F to 375°F for 30 to 45 minutes will work!

SIDES

Mock Mashed Potatoes

Calories: 140 | Fat: 11g | Protein: 5g | Fiber: 3g | **Net Carbs: 4g**

Doing without your favorite foods simply won't do, as that's something absolutely unheard of in the Stella home! For instance, we found a new favorite when we substituted that nameless high-carb root vegetable with healthy and light, yet filling, cauliflower. And even better, we piled them high with the best ingredients we could find!

SHOPPING LIST

1 medium head cauliflower

1 tablespoon cream cheese, softened

¼ cup grated Parmesan cheese

¼ teaspoon minced fresh garlic

¼ teaspoon chicken base or bouillon

⅛ teaspoon black pepper

½ teaspoon chopped fresh or dried chives, for garnish

3 tablespoons unsalted butter, if desired

HELPFUL HINTS

The chicken base or bouillon adds a lot of flavor to these "potatoes," but you can skip it if you prefer—just be sure to season with salt to taste to replace the salt in the bouillon.

1 BRING a large pot of water to a boil over high heat.

2 CLEAN and cut cauliflower into small pieces. Add to the pot and boil for about 6 minutes until well done.

3 DRAIN well but do not let cool. Pat the cooked cauliflower between several layers of paper towels or place cauliflower in a colander and use a heavy bowl to press down on it to remove the excess water.

4 USING a food processor or hand blender, pulse the hot cauliflower with the cream cheese, Parmesan, garlic, chicken base, and pepper until almost smooth.

5 GARNISH with chives and serve hot with pats of butter, if desired.

SIDES

Eggplant, Yellow Squash, and Tomato Casino

Calories: 135 | Fat: 7.5g | Protein: 7g | Fiber: 3g | **Net Carbs: 4g**

Baked vegetables are a favorite of mine, especially when there are a variety of colors involved. These eggplants, yellow squash, and tomatoes are topped with vibrant bell peppers, real bacon bits, and Parmesan cheese for maximum jackpot flavor!

SHOPPING LIST

2 small eggplants

2 yellow squash, small to medium size

4 Roma tomatoes

Kosher salt

Black pepper

Garlic powder

2 tablespoons real bacon bits

1 tablespoon finely diced red bell pepper

1 tablespoon finely diced green bell pepper

1 tablespoon finely diced red onion

¾ cup grated Parmesan cheese

2 tablespoons extra-virgin olive oil

1 PREHEAT oven to 350°F.

2 CUT the ends off both eggplants and the yellow squash, and then slice each in half lengthwise. Lay cut sides up and close together on a small greased sheet pan.

3 CUT the tops and a very small piece of the bottom off the Roma tomatoes and stand them up on the pan alongside the halved vegetables.

4 SPRINKLE liberally with salt, pepper, garlic powder, bacon bits, red and green bell peppers, and onion.

5 CAREFULLY pile high the Parmesan over each piece, drizzle with olive oil, and bake for about 12 minutes, or until the cheese begins to turn golden brown. Serve immediately.

HELPFUL HINTS

Japanese eggplants work best in this recipe, as they are naturally small and cook in about the same time as the other vegetables.

SIDES

Roasted Cajun Cauliflower

Calories: 90 | Fat: 7g | Protein: 2.5g | Fiber: 3.5g | **Net Carbs: 3.5g**

Cajun spices are quite universal in that you can use the same seasoning combination with almost any type of ingredients—from meat, poultry, or seafood to vegetables like in this recipe. If you have some of my Blackening Spice (see page: 153) on hand, simply use 2 teaspoons of that in place of the spices in this recipe and you're already there!

SHOPPING LIST

Vegetable oil spray

1 medium head cauliflower, cored and thickly chopped

2 tablespoons olive oil

1 teaspoon kosher salt

½ teaspoon cumin

½ teaspoon dried thyme

¼ teaspoon black pepper

¼ teaspoon garlic powder

⅛ teaspoon cayenne pepper

1 PREHEAT the oven to 425°F and spray a sheet pan with vegetable oil spray.

2 IN a large bowl, combine all ingredients and mix well to coat.

3 TRANSFER the seasoned cauliflower to a sheet pan and spread out in a single layer.

4 BAKE for about 20 minutes, just until tender and starting to brown. Serve garnished with diced roasted red peppers or tomatoes, if desired.

HELPFUL HINTS

This side dish looks fantastic served in the center of a white platter with blackening spice or paprika sprinkled around the edges!

SIDES

Grilled Baked Apples

Calories: 120 | Fat: 6g | Protein: 0.5g | Fiber: 2.5g | **Net Carbs: 13.5g**

I used to go apple picking with my father in Connecticut, as apples were his favorite snack. I can still hear him saying, "An apple a day keeps the doctor away," every single time he picked an apple! As a kid, I had no idea how true that statement would turn out to be. Warm baked apples were always a treat on a cold night, but now that we live in a warmer climate, which allows us to grill often, we find it easy to just put these on the shelf in the grill while our dinner and veggies cook over the main flame below!

SHOPPING LIST

4 large Gala or red apples

2 tablespoons bulk sugar substitute (recommended: Splenda)

1 teaspoon ground cinnamon

4 drops vanilla extract

2 tablespoons butter, melted (may use light, trans-fat free buttery spread)

HELPFUL HINTS

I always use "heavy-duty" aluminum foil when grilling, as I've actually seen the thinner aluminum foils melt in the flame!

1 CAREFULLY remove the apple cores without cutting all the way through to the bottom of the apple.

2 COMBINE the remaining ingredients and pour an equal amount of the mixture into each cored apple.

3 SET each of the filled apples in the center of a large piece of heavy-duty aluminum foil, pull the sides up, and twist at the top to completely seal inside. If not completely sealed, wrap in a second piece of foil.

4 PLACE wrapped apples in a roasting pan and place on a shelf inside your grill. Close grill and let cook 15 minutes, or until apples feel soft. You may also bake in an oven at 400°F for about 15 minutes, if desired. Serve warm.

SIDES

Spinach Ricotta Casserole

Calories: 105 | Fat: 6g | Protein: 9.5g | Fiber: 1g | **Net Carbs: 2.5g**

Ricotta, mozzarella, and Parmesan—now that's what I call the "perfecta trifecta" of Italian cheese casserole medleys! Throw in a whole bunch of spinach and now we're talking! You don't have to "Rome" far from home to get a taste of what Italy's all about.

SHOPPING LIST

Vegetable oil spray

16 ounces frozen chopped spinach, thawed and well drained

1 ½ cups ricotta cheese

½ cup shredded mozzarella cheese

¼ cup grated Parmesan cheese

6 large eggs, beaten until frothy

1 teaspoon Dijon mustard

½ teaspoon Italian seasoning

¼ teaspoon garlic powder

¼ teaspoon kosher salt

⅛ teaspoon black pepper

HELPFUL HINTS

Try adding ¼ cup diced bell peppers to the casserole before baking for extra color and flavor!

1 PREHEAT the oven to 350°F. Spray a 1 ½ quart casserole dish with vegetable oil and layer the bottom evenly with the drained spinach.

2 IN a bowl, mix the remaining ingredients until combined. Pour mixture into the spinach lined dish.

3 BAKE for 35 to 40 minutes, until slightly browned around the edges and center is firm to touch. Serve warm, garnished with fresh basil and diced tomatoes, if desired.

SIDES

DESERTS

| Prep Time 30 min | Cook Time 1:45 min | Serves 12 |

Stella Style Ricotta Cheesecake

Calories: 270 | Fat: 24g | Protein: 8.5g | Fiber: 0g | **Net Carbs: 4g**

This is a completely updated version of the cheesecake that literally got me my show on the Food Network. I snuck it into their offices and the rest is history! Of course, Rachel deserves all the credit, because, as with most baked goods in this book, she has spent years perfecting it. Not only is this cheesecake even more dense and creamy than ever before, but it is also baked in far less time!

SHOPPING LIST

Vegetable oil spray

24 ounces cream cheese, softened

1 cup extra-fine ricotta cheese (see hints)

1 ½ cups bulk sugar substitute (recommended: Splenda)

⅓ cup heavy cream

1 tablespoon pure vanilla extract

1 tablespoon fresh lemon juice

2 large eggs

3 large egg yolks

PLACE the oven rack in the center position and preheat to 400°F. Spray an 8-inch springform pan with vegetable oil spray.

WRAP the entire outside of the springform pan in aluminum foil to prevent any water from seeping into the cake.

MAKE a water bath so the top of the cheesecake won't split as it bakes: Pour about 1 inch hot water into a shallow roasting pan big enough to hold the cake pan and place it on the center rack of the oven to heat.

WITH an electric mixer on low speed, beat the cream cheese, ricotta, and sugar substitute for about 1 minute, until well blended.

IN a separate bowl, whisk the cream, vanilla, lemon juice, eggs, and egg yolks until blended.

TURN the mixer on medium speed and slowly pour the egg mixture into the cream cheese mixture. Beat just until blended; be careful not to over-whip.

POUR the batter into the greased springform pan and smooth the top with a spatula. Place the pan in the heated water bath and bake for 15 minutes.

LOWER the oven temperature to 325°F. Continue baking for about 1 ½ hours, until the top is a light golden brown and the cake is pulling away from the sides of the pan.

REMOVE from oven and let cool on counter for 1 hour, and then refrigerate at least 8 hours before slicing to serve.

HELPFUL HINTS

We usually process the ricotta cheese with a hand-blender or food processor until it is nearly as smooth as sour cream. It only takes about a minute and helps make for the smoothest cake.

DESSERTS

Chocolate Marble Ricotta Cake

Calories: 150 | Fat: 12g | Protein: 8g | Fiber: 2.5g | **Net Carbs: 4g**

Even I was shocked by how beautiful Rachel was able to make this marbled cake. Of course, that shock was soon replaced by the shock of just how delicious it was! Adding ricotta to the batter gives it a real richness that is surprisingly low in not only carbs but calories too.

SHOPPING LIST

Vegetable oil spray

6 large eggs, beaten until frothy

1 ¼ cups whole milk ricotta cheese

½ teaspoon vanilla extract

1 teaspoon almond extract

2 ⅓ cups almond flour

1 ¼ cups bulk sugar substitute (recommended: Splenda)

1 ½ teaspoons baking powder

⅓ cup unsweetened cocoa powder

2 tablespoons butter, melted

HELPFUL HINTS

For a uniform and clean look, make the almond flour from blanched almonds without the brown skins.

1 PREHEAT oven to 325°F. Spray a 9x5 loaf pan with vegetable oil spray and then line with parchment paper.

2 IN an electric mixer on high speed, beat eggs, ricotta cheese, vanilla extract, and almond extract until well combined with no clumps.

3 CHANGE the mixer to medium speed and add the almond flour, sugar substitute, and baking powder. Mix until all is combined into a batter.

4 IN a separate mixing bowl, whisk together cocoa powder and melted butter. Add half of the cake batter to the cocoa mixture and mix well to create a chocolate batter.

5 POUR both the regular and chocolate batters into the prepared loaf pan and use a butter knife to (very) gently swirl the two together, creating a marbling effect.

6 BAKE 1 hour, or until top is golden brown and a toothpick inserted into the center comes out mostly clean. Cool completely before removing from the pan. Slice into 8 thick slices and cut each slice in half to make 16 portions. Serve chilled.

DESSERTS

Homemade Ricotta Cheese

Calories: 90 | Fat: 6.5g | Protein: 4g | Fiber: 0g | **Net Carbs: 4g**

There is something purely magical about watching milk and cream transform into a cheese delicacy before your very eyes. We make a lot of our own condiments at home, so even though this is simple to pick up at a grocery store, it's always best fresh. Besides, ricotta is also quick and fun to make—especially when kids decide to help! Makes about 2 cups.

SHOPPING LIST

2 quarts whole milk

1 cup heavy cream

¼ cup fresh lemon juice

1 tablespoon salt

SPECIAL EQUIPMENT

Candy thermometer

Cheesecloth or fine mesh strainer

HELPFUL HINTS

When ricotta is made from scratch like this, it should be savored and served with fresh berries and nuts. We typically use the store bought kind when ricotta is called for in complicated baking recipes.

1 PLACE a deep, heavy pot over medium-high heat and then add the milk and cream. While stirring, use a candy thermometer to monitor as you bring the mixture to a temperature of 190°F.

2 QUICKLY stir in the lemon juice and salt and cook for 1 to 2 minutes more, until curds form.

3 REMOVE the pot from heat and spoon out curds into a fine mesh strainer (or a regular one lined with cheesecloth). Once completely drained, refrigerate curds for at least 2 hours to firm.

DESSERTS

Pecan Ganache Macaroons

Calories: 75 | Fat: 6.5g | Protein: 2g | Fiber: 1g | **Net Carbs: 1g**

These coconut macaroons are not only filled with finely ground pecans but are also topped with homemade Chocolate Ganache. Makes 24 macaroons.

SHOPPING LIST

4 large egg whites, cold

1 ½ teaspoons vanilla extract

¼ teaspoon cream of tartar

½ cup bulk sugar substitute (recommended: Splenda)

½ cup pecans, finely ground (may use almond flour)

½ cup unsweetened shredded coconut

CHOCOLATE GANACHE

1 tablespoon butter

½ cup bulk sugar substitute

2 teaspoons half and half, may use heavy cream

1 ounce unsweetened baking chocolate, chopped

1 teaspoon vanilla extract

HELPFUL HINTS

If the Chocolate Ganache is too thick, thin it out with a little extra half and half.

1 PREHEAT the oven to 325°F and line a sheet pan with parchment paper.

2 ADD the egg whites to a mixing bowl and whisk until frothy. Add the vanilla extract, cream of tartar, and sugar substitute, and whisk until a little more frothy and thick. Fold in the ground pecans and coconut until well combined.

3 PLACE heaping tablespoons of the meringue mixture in rows on the lined sheet pan, leaving a space between each cookie. Press the center of each cookie down lightly, leaving an impression to fill with the Ganache after baking.

4 BAKE for 25 minutes, or until they start to brown and are slightly firm to the touch. Cool completely.

5 WHILE the Ganache is still warm (see below), spoon a small amount inside the thumb impression in the center of each baked cookie. Serve cookies at room temperature.

1 **To make the Chocolate Ganache:** Fill a pot over medium-high heat with 2 inches of water and bring to a low simmer. Place a stainless steel bowl over the pot.

2 ADD the butter, sugar substitute, and half and half to the bowl and mix with a spatula until combined.

3 ADD the chopped chocolate and stir just until melted and combined. Remove from heat and stir in the vanilla.

DESSERTS

Peanut Butter Brownie Minis

Calories: 90 | Fat: 8.5g | Protein: 3g | Fiber: 2g | **Net Carbs: 1g**

These mini (and flourless!) brownie bites are topped with a homemade peanut butter frosting to take them to a whole 'nother level. Makes 24 pieces.

SHOPPING LIST

Vegetable oil spray

¼ cup + 2 tablespoons half and half

2 ounces unsweetened baking chocolate, chopped

4 tablespoons butter, softened

1 cup bulk sugar substitute (recommended: Splenda)

½ teaspoon vanilla extract

2 large eggs

1 large egg yolk

2 tablespoons unsweetened cocoa powder

¾ cup milled flax seed

1 teaspoon baking powder

2 tablespoons water

PEANUT BUTTER FROSTING

1 tablespoon butter, softened

2 ounces cream cheese, softened

⅓ cup natural creamy peanut butter

⅓ cup bulk sugar substitute

½ teaspoon vanilla extract

HELPFUL HINTS

Be careful to bake the brownies just until firm, as over-baking them will dry them out.

1 SPRAY a 24-count mini muffin pan with vegetable oil spray. Place oven rack in the center position and preheat to 350°F.

2 FILL a pot with 2 inches of water and place over medium-high heat, bringing to a very low simmer. Place a stainless steel bowl over the pot (above the water) to create a double boiler.

3 ADD ¼ cup of the half and half and all of the baking chocolate to the stainless steel bowl, mixing with a rubber spatula for about 2 minutes until chocolate is melted and mixture is creamy. Set aside to cool down.

4 PLACE butter in an electric mixer and beat on high speed until fluffy, about 2 to 3 minutes. Add sugar substitute, vanilla extract, and remaining half and half, and then continue beating as you add the eggs and egg yolk one at a time.

5 STOP the mixer and add the cocoa powder, milled flax seed, baking powder, water, and the melted chocolate mixture. Restart the mixer on low and mix well, about another 2 minutes.

6 FILL each muffin cup with an equal amount of the brownie batter. (A one ounce ice cream scoop works best.) Bake 15 to 20 minutes just until a toothpick comes out mostly clean.

7 COOL Brownie Minis completely before whisking together all frosting ingredients and spreading over top. Serve chilled for best taste.

DESSERTS

Spiced Whoopie Pies

Calories: 270 | Fat: 26g | Protein: 6g | Fiber: 2g | **Net Carbs: 2g**

Christian told us that Whoopie Pies were the new BIG thing, so naturally Rachel and I set out to reinvent them in a low carb way. Since we made them on Thanksgiving, we decided to spice them up a bit and the results were delicious! Makes 8 Whoopie Pies.

SHOPPING LIST

2 ounces cream cheese, softened

2 tablespoons butter, softened

¾ cup bulk sugar substitute (recommended: Splenda)

1 large egg

1 teaspoon vanilla extract

1 cup almond flour

½ teaspoon baking soda

½ teaspoon pumpkin pie spice

⅓ cup chopped pecans

FILLING

3 tablespoons butter, softened

6 ounces cream cheese, softened

½ cup bulk sugar substitute (recommended: Splenda)

1 teaspoon vanilla extract

HELPFUL HINTS

You can make your own pumpkin pie spice by mixing 3 tablespoons ground cinnamon, 3 teaspoons ground ginger, 2 teaspoons ground nutmeg, and 1 teaspoon allspice. Only use ½ teaspoon of the finished spice in this recipe though!

1 PREHEAT oven to 350°F and line a sheet pan with parchment paper.

2 PLACE cream cheese, butter, sugar substitute, egg, and vanilla extract in an electric mixer and beat on high until fluffy.

3 ADD the almond flour, baking soda, pumpkin pie spice, and pecans, and beat on medium, just until all is combined into a thin dough.

4 USING a spoon or a 1-ounce ice cream scoop, drop 16 evenly spaced dollops of the dough onto the prepared sheet pan and press down lightly to flatten.

5 BAKE 8 to 10 minutes, until cookies are springy in the center. Let cool at least 15 minutes.

6 MEANWHILE, beat all Filling ingredients in an electric mixer on high until well combined.

7 SPREAD a thick layer of the Filling in between 2 finished cookies to make a Whoopie Pie. Repeat with all remaining cookies. Chill at least 4 hours before serving.

DESSERTS

French Vanilla Pudding

Calories: 160 | Fat: 14g | Protein: 4g | Fiber: 0g | **Net Carbs: 4.5g**

Gotta love the art of French cooking! Why? Because from one simple technique, many recipes are born! This one uses the French style of thickening by cooking egg yolks and cream, which is a perfect low carb way to work around the fact that every recipe for pudding ever written normally includes forbidden corn starch as a thickener. Once you've gotten the hang of preparing this pudding, you can then try your hand at ice cream or baked custard using the same ingredients and methods!

SHOPPING LIST

3 cups half and half

1 packet plain gelatin (recommended: Knoxx brand)

¾ cup bulk sugar substitute (recommended: Splenda)

4 large egg yolks, beaten

2 teaspoons vanilla extract, no sugar added

1 tablespoon butter

HELPFUL HINTS

French vanilla ice cream, or Crème Anglaise, is easily made by increasing the egg yolks to 8, eliminating the gelatin and butter, and churning the mixture in an ice cream churner until frozen and smooth.

For custard, mix the cold cream, 6 eggs, sugar substitute, and vanilla together. Pour the mixture into oven-proof bowls and bake in a shallow water bath at 375°F for about 30 minutes. Serve hot or chilled.

1 ADD ¼ cup of the cold half and half cream to a small bowl, sprinkle the packet of gelatin over it, and set aside.

2 PLACE remaining cream and sugar substitute in a small saucepan over medium-high heat and stir constantly, until simmering.

3 REMOVE from heat and quickly stir about 1 cup of the hot cream into the bowl with the egg yolks and another ½ cup of the cream into the bowl with the gelatin.

4 ADD the cream and egg yolk mixture back to the sauce pan over the heat and stir constantly for about 5 minutes, or until sauce begins to thicken slightly.

5 REMOVE from heat, stir in the vanilla, butter, and dissolved gelatin, and pour into 8 small dishes. Chill for at least 3 to 4 hours before devouring!

DESSERTS

Italian Almond Cake

Calories: 150 | Fat: 12g | Protein: 7g | Fiber: 2.5g | **Net Carbs: 3g**

"King" cakes like this one are a tradition in northern Italy where my father's family was from. My mother often made it when relatives would visit, and while the adults played cards and sipped coffee, my cousins and I would sneak some cake! Of course, she was smart enough to know what we were up to, because why else would she make 3 cakes?

SHOPPING LIST

Vegetable oil spray

5 large eggs

2 teaspoons vanilla extract

1 teaspoon almond extract

2 tablespoons fresh lemon juice

1 tablespoon lemon zest

2 ½ cups almond flour

¾ cup bulk sugar substitute (recommended: Splenda)

1 tablespoon baking powder

HELPFUL HINTS

To doubly ensure the cake will easily release from the pan, Rachel says to simply line the bottom of your pan with parchment paper before spraying with vegetable oil for a quick release every time!

1 PLACE oven rack in the center position, preheat to 350°F, and spray an 8-inch round cake pan with vegetable oil.

2 IN a large bowl, beat eggs until frothy. Add the extracts, lemon juice and zest, and ¼ cup of tap water to the bowl and beat to combine.

3 IN another bowl, mix the almond flour, sugar substitute, and baking powder, and then beat this dry ingredient mixture into the egg mixture until all are combined.

4 POUR the finished batter into the prepared cake pan and bake 30 to 35 minutes, or until center is firm and springy. A toothpick inserted into the center should come out clean.

5 COOL on a wire rack for 30 minutes and refrigerate for at least 2 hours before turning pan upside down and shaking to release the cake.

DESSERTS

Strawberry Cheesecake Crumble

NO

Calories: 190 | Fat: 15.5g | Protein: 8g | Fiber: 1.5g | **Net Carbs: 4g**

This Strawberry Cheesecake Crumble is amazingly decadent yet only has 4 grams of net carbs and under 200 calories! With a cake layer stuffed with strawberries, a cheesecake layer, and then a crumble... this simply can't get any better.

SHOPPING LIST

4 large eggs

½ cup heavy cream

½ cup water

2 teaspoons vanilla extract

1 cup soy flour

½ cup bulk sugar substitute (recommended: Splenda)

2 teaspoons baking powder

⅔ cup sliced strawberries

8 ounces cream cheese, softened

CRUMBLE

3 tablespoons butter, softened

½ cup almond flour

¼ cup bulk sugar substitute

½ teaspoon ground cinnamon

HELPFUL HINTS

Careful not to over mix the Crumble Topping as it can quickly become too smooth.

1 PLACE oven rack in the center position and preheat to 375°F. Line an 8x8-inch baking dish with parchment paper.

2 ADD 3 of the 4 eggs to a bowl with the heavy cream, water, and vanilla extract, and whisk until frothy. Stir in soy flour, ½ cup bulk sugar substitute, and baking powder.

3 FOLD in half of the sliced strawberries and pour the mix into the prepared pan.

4 IN another mixing bowl, combine the cream cheese and remaining egg, and spread evenly over the batter in the pan. Top with the remaining strawberry slices.

5 IN another bowl, combine the crumble ingredients and crumble over the top of the cake.

6 BAKE for 40 minutes, or until a toothpick inserted comes out mostly clean. Let cool for 10 minutes before slicing into 12 pieces and serving warm or cold.

DESSERT

Chocolate Pecan Cheesecake Squares

Calories: 195 | Fat: 17.5g | Protein: 6g | Fiber: 1g | **Net Carbs: 2.5g**

Just how could we improve on our famous no-sugar cheesecake? Putting it on an almond crust and topping with chocolate and pecans... that's definitely one way!

SHOPPING LIST

CRUST

2 large eggs, beaten until frothy

1 cup almond flour

⅓ cup bulk sugar substitute

1 teaspoon baking powder

FILLING

16 ounces cream cheese, softened

½ cup bulk sugar substitute

1 tablespoon vanilla extract

3 large eggs

1 batch Chocolate Ganache (recipe included on page: 193)

16 pecan halves

HELPFUL HINTS

We use 2 pieces of parchment paper to ensure that the sides of the baking dish are entirely covered.

1 PLACE oven rack in the center position and preheat to 350°F. Line an 8x8-inch baking dish with parchment paper.

2 ADD crust ingredients to a bowl and mix well. Spread into the lined baking dish and bake for about 15 minutes, or until lightly browned. Remove and let cool for 5 minutes.

3 AS the crust bakes, add the filling ingredients to an electric mixer and mix on medium speed for just 1 minute.

4 POUR over the pre-baked crust in the baking dish and bake for about 30 minutes, or until the center is firm and a toothpick inserted comes out mostly clean. Let cool 30 minutes.

5 WHILE the cake is cooling, prepare the Chocolate Ganache and quickly drizzle over the top of the cake—sticking the pecan halves in rows into the chocolate.

6 REFRIGERATE for at least 2 hours before removing entire cake from pan by lifting the parchment paper out. Slice into 16 squares to serve.

DESSERTS

Praline Pumpkin Pie

Calories: 130 | Fat: 11.5g | Protein: 3g | Fiber: 1.5g | **Net Carbs: 2.5g**

This is an updated version of one of the very first desserts Rachel created after we started on our low carb lifestyle. By recreating an absolutely delicious pumpkin pie, she ensured that we would never go through the holidays without a sweet tradition.

SHOPPING LIST

CRUST

2 tablespoons butter

½ cup finely chopped pecans

½ cup bulk sugar substitute (recommended: Splenda)

⅛ teaspoon salt

⅛ teaspoon ground cinnamon

FILLING

1 (15-ounce) can pure pumpkin (not pumpkin pie filling)

¾ cup bulk sugar substitute (recommended: Splenda)

1 tablespoon plus a dash more pumpkin pie spice

1 ¼ cups heavy cream

4 large eggs

HELPFUL HINTS

While we often whip our own, most grocery stores now carry real "no sugar added" whipped heavy cream in a can (Land-O-Lakes brand).

1 PREHEAT the oven to 350°F.

2 To make the crust, melt the butter in a small saucepan or in the microwave and mix all the crust ingredients together in a small bowl.

3 WHILE the mixture is still warm from the butter, press it down evenly over the bottom of a 10-inch deep pie pan. Bake for about 5 minutes, until browned, and remove the crust from the oven. Turn the oven up to 425°F.

4 To make the filling, place all the filling ingredients in a medium bowl and whisk together.

5 POUR the filling into the crust. Bake for 15 minutes, and then reduce the heat to 350°F. Continue to bake for an additional 50 to 55 minutes until done. (To test for doneness, stick a toothpick in the center; if it comes out clean, the pie is done.) Cool on the counter for at least 30 minutes, and then chill for at least 3 hours before serving. Try serving with a dollop of sugar-free whipped cream.

DESSERTS

Cannoli Parfaits

Calories: 200 | Fat: 19g | Protein: 4g | Fiber: 1g | **Net Carbs: 4g**

I've always loved cannolis, but it wasn't until I was living a low carb lifestyle that I realized how unnecessary the high-carb cannoli shell really is! These parfaits, stuffed with chunks of homemade chocolate, are served in a glass and eaten with a spoon—something that actually makes them into a nicer dessert for entertaining.

SHOPPING LIST

CHOCOLATE CHUNKS

1 tablespoon butter

½ cup bulk sugar substitute

2 teaspoons half and half, may use heavy cream

1 ounce unsweetened baking chocolate, chopped

PARFAITS

1 cup heavy cream

⅓ cup bulk sugar substitute (recommended: Splenda)

1 teaspoon vanilla extract

¼ teaspoon almond extract

⅓ cup ricotta cheese

HELPFUL HINTS

You can also make these with toasted almond slivers in place of the chocolate chunks for Toasted Almond Parfaits.

1 FILL a pot over medium-high heat with 2 inches of water and bring to a low simmer. Place a stainless steel bowl over the pot.

2 ADD the butter, sugar substitute, and half and half to the bowl and mix with a spatula until combined.

3 ADD the chopped chocolate and stir just until melted and combined. Remove from heat and spread on a plate covered with waxed paper. Freeze for about 15 minutes before breaking into small chunks.

4 WITH an electric mixer on high speed, whip the cream just until frothy. Add the sugar substitute and extracts, and then whip on high speed until soft peaks form. Be careful not to over-whip, or the whipped cream will break down.

5 USE a spoon to gently fold in the ricotta cheese and most of the chocolate chunks, saving a few for garnish.

6 SPOON the cannoli cream into 4 parfait glasses, top with the remaining chocolate chunks, and refrigerate for at least 1 hour before serving.

DESSERTS

Lemon Mascarpone Flan

Calories: 135 | Fat: 10g | Protein: 7.5g | Fiber: 0g | **Net Carbs: 2.5g**

These mini flan cups are a quick "chef's dessert" that gets a nice, but not overbearing tartness from lemon juice and zest. I say this is a "chef's dessert" because it is so easy that it is usually something we chefs fall back on because we are totally mystified by the art of baking. (That's why I have Rachel!)

SHOPPING LIST

Vegetable oil spray

4 large eggs

4 ounces mascarpone cheese, softened (may use cream cheese)

1 cup half and half

1 teaspoon vanilla extract

3 tablespoons fresh lemon juice

1 teaspoon minced lemon zest

⅓ cup bulk sugar substitute (recommended: Splenda)

1 ADD 1 inch of water to a shallow roasting pan to make a water bath. Place on the center rack of oven and preheat to 350°F.

2 SPRAY six small custard cups or 6-ounce rame-kins with vegetable oil spray.

3 ADD the eggs to a mixing bowl and beat with a wire whisk until frothy. Add all the remaining ingredients and beat until well combined.

4 POUR equal amounts of the mix into each of the 6 prepared cups and place into the preheated water bath. Bake for about 45 minutes, until firm and a toothpick inserted in the center comes out clean.

5 COOL on the counter for 1 hour before refrigerating for at least 3 additional hours. Serve cold, topped with sugar-free whipped cream and lemon zest, if desired.

HELPFUL HINTS

You can also make this flan with tangerine or key lime juices and zests for completely different flavors.

DESSERTS

Meringue Clouds

Calories: 10 | Fat: 0g | Protein: 1.5g | Fiber: 0g | **Net Carbs: 0g**

These fluffy, light, low carb delights are not only light in your hand but also on your hips. With only 10 calories per 3 cookies, you are sure to be on cloud nine! Makes about 30 cookies.

SHOPPING LIST

4 large egg whites, cold

½ teaspoon vanilla extract

¼ teaspoon cream of tartar

¼ cup bulk sugar substitute

HELPFUL HINTS

Try replacing the vanilla extract with coconut extract for an entirely different cookie!

1 PREHEAT the oven to 325°F and spray a cookie sheet with vegetable oil.

2 ADD the egg whites to a mixing bowl and beat on highest speed just until frothy, about 1 minute. Add all the remaining ingredients and beat on high until soft peaks form.

3 PLACE heaping tablespoons of the meringue in rows on the sprayed sheet pan, leaving a couple inches of space between each cookie. The recipe should make about 30 cookies.

4 BAKE for about 45 minutes until just starting to brown and getting firm to the touch. Remove and cool completely before serving. Store unrefrigerated in a covered container.

DESSERTS

Pumpkin Applesauce Cake

Calories: 195 | Fat: 15.5g | Protein: 7g | Fiber: 3g | **Net Carbs: 5.5g**

This spiced cake with buttercream frosting is great to make around the holidays. With puréed pumpkin, applesauce, and the natural moisture of almond flour... this cake is about as moist as it gets.

SHOPPING LIST

Vegetable oil spray

8 large eggs

2 cups canned pure pumpkin

1 ½ cups unsweetened applesauce

2 teaspoons vanilla extract

3 cups almond flour

1 cup bulk sugar substitute (recommended: Splenda)

2 teaspoons baking powder

2 teaspoons pumpkin pie spice

¼ teaspoon ground cinnamon

FROSTING

3 tablespoons butter, softened

6 ounces cream cheese, softened

½ cup bulk sugar substitute (recommended: Splenda)

1 teaspoon vanilla extract

1 PLACE oven rack in center position and preheat to 350°F. Spray a 13x9-inch baking dish with vegetable oil spray.

2 IN a large mixing bowl, beat eggs until frothy. Stir in pumpkin, applesauce, and vanilla extract, and beat until fully combined.

3 ADD all remaining ingredients, except frosting ingredients, to the bowl and mix well to create a batter.

4 POUR batter in the prepared baking dish and spread out evenly. Bake 50 to 60 minutes, or until a toothpick inserted into the center comes out mostly clean.

5 MEANWHILE, beat all Frosting ingredients in an electric mixer on high until well combined.

6 LET cake cool at least 15 minutes before frosting. Slice into 18 squares to serve.

HELPFUL HINTS

While this is good warm, we prefer it chilled for at least 3 to 4 hours before serving.

DESSERTS

French Meringue Macaroons

Calories: 115 | Fat: 10.5g | Protein: 4g | Fiber: 1g | **Net Carbs: 1.5g**

Almond flour truly works its magic in these fluffy, sweet, French cookies. The frosting on the cake (or on the cookie in this case) is the cream cheese filling! Makes 12 stuffed cookies.

SHOPPING LIST

4 large egg whites, cold

½ teaspoon coconut extract

¼ teaspoon cream of tartar

¼ cup bulk sugar substitute (recommended: Splenda)

1 cup almond flour, finely ground

FILLING

6 ounces cream cheese, softened to room temperature

2 tablespoons butter, softened to room temperature

⅓ cup bulk sugar substitute (recommended: Splenda)

1 teaspoon coconut extract (may use vanilla)

HELPFUL HINTS

Try adding food coloring or unsweetened cocoa powder to the cookies and filling to create unique cookies as pictured at left.

1 PREHEAT the oven to 325°F and line a cookie sheet with parchment paper.

2 ADD the egg whites to a mixing bowl and whisk until frothy. Add all the remaining ingredients, except the almond flour, and whisk until a little more frothy and thick.

3 FOLD in the almond flour until well combined. Place heaping tablespoons of the meringue mixture in rows on the prepared sheet pan, leaving a couple inches of space between each cookie. The recipe should make about 24 cookies.

4 BAKE for about 25 minutes, until just starting to brown and they are firm to the touch. Remove and cool completely before frosting.

5 WHILE the meringue cookies cool, make the filling by adding all of the filling ingredients to an electric mixer and beating on the highest speed until light and fluffy.

6 NOTE: Only frost right before serving. To serve, spread a thin layer of filling between 2 cooled baked cookies to make the meringue macaroons. Serve immediately once frosted; otherwise, store unfrosted cookies in an airtight container on the counter, keeping the filling in the refrigerator.

DESSERTS

Pumpkin Pound Cake

Calories: 130 | Fat: 9.5g | Protein: 6g | Fiber: 2.5g | **Net Carbs: 4.5g**

This pound cake has become THE holiday staple in the Stella household. I simply cannot remember a single holiday meal where Rachel did not prepare this since she first came up with it over 6 years ago. Over time, she has absolutely perfected this moist, holiday-spiced cake and even managed to cut the cooking time down by 30 minutes!

SHOPPING LIST

Vegetable oil spray

2 ½ cups almond flour

1 ½ cups bulk sugar substitute (recommended: Splenda)

1 ½ teaspoons baking powder

1 ½ teaspoons pumpkin pie spice

¼ teaspoon salt

7 large eggs

1 ½ cups canned pure pumpkin (not pumpkin pie filling)

1 ½ teaspoons vanilla extract

HELPFUL HINTS

For best results, use a silicone loaf pan to prevent sticking. Or do what Rachel does and line a traditional loaf pan with parchment paper.

1 PREHEAT the oven to 325°F.

2 HEAVILY spray a 9x5 loaf pan with vegetable oil spray.

3 IN a large mixing bowl, whisk together the almond flour, sugar substitute, baking powder, pumpkin pie spice, and salt.

4 IN another bowl, beat the eggs, and then whisk in the pumpkin and vanilla. Combine the dry and wet ingredients and stir until combined.

5 POUR the batter into the prepared pan. Bake until golden brown and a toothpick comes out clean when stuck in the center, about 1 hour. Cool completely before removing from the pan. Slice into 8 thick slices and cut each slice in half to make 16 portions. Serve warm or chilled.

Almond Flour

Calories: 140 | Fat: 12g | Protein: 5g | Fiber: 3g | **Net Carbs: 2g**

While many may think that using ground almonds in place of white flour in baked goods adds unnecessary fat—it is important to note that the fat in almonds is the "good" monounsaturated fat that I am sure you have heard about by now. I can't reiterate this enough—almonds are natural and very, very good for you! So while you may balk at the fat grams of some of the recipes in this book that include almond flour, studies have shown that adding almonds to your diet can actually increase weight loss! It is also important to note that since we first started grinding raw almonds into flour nearly a decade ago, we have realized that sliced almonds grind much faster and more easily than the whole almonds we used to recommend.

SHOPPING LIST

10 ounces sliced raw almonds (may use whole raw almonds)

HELPFUL HINTS

For the absolutely smoothest and most flour-like consistency, start the almonds by grinding them in a food processor and then run them (in small batches) through a coffee grinder. This is good for recipes where a smoother texture is expected, as with cookies, but we honestly don't do this very often ourselves!

1 GRIND the almonds on high in a food processor for about 3 minutes, until they've reached a grainy, flour-like consistency.

2 ALMOND flour can be stored in an airtight container for up to 1 week on the counter or for several months in the freezer.

DESSERTS

Joyous Almond Cups

Calories: 70 | Fat: 7g | Protein: 1.5g | Fiber: 1.5g | **Net Carbs: 1g**

These satisfying chocolate cups taste just like a coconut and almond chocolate bar. The big secret is that they don't even contain any coconut! Makes 20 Joyous Almond Cups.

SHOPPING LIST

CHOCOLATE CUPS

4 tablespoons butter

1 ½ cups bulk sugar substitute (recommended: Splenda)

2 tablespoons half and half

4 ounces unsweetened baking chocolate, chopped

COCONUT CENTER

⅓ cup almond flour

¼ cup bulk sugar substitute (recommended: Splenda)

1 ounce cream cheese, softened

⅛ teaspoon coconut extract

¼ cup sliced almonds

HELPFUL HINTS

The Coconut Center should be thick and doughy. If too thin, add a tablespoon or 2 of additional almond flour to thicken it up.

1 ARRANGE 20 mini paper cupcake liners in a mini muffin pan, on a sheet pan, or in a large rectangular baking dish.

2 FILL a pot with 2 inches of water and place over medium-high heat, bringing water to a very low simmer. Place a stainless steel bowl over the pot (above the water) to create a double boiler.

3 ADD the butter, sugar substitute, and half and half to the stainless steel bowl, mixing with a rubber spatula until butter is melted and well combined.

4 ADD the chopped unsweetened chocolate and slowly stir for about 2 minutes, just until melted and combined with the other ingredients. Remove from heat and pour an equal amount into each of the 20 cupcake liners, filling each about half way.

5 IN a mixing bowl, combine all Coconut Center ingredients, except sliced almonds, and mix with a fork.

6 FORM the Center ingredients into 20 equal-sized balls, and using the back of a spoon, press each into the center of a chocolate cup.

7 TOP the filled chocolate cups with sliced almonds and refrigerate at least 3 hours, until firm.

DESSERTS

Dark Chocolate Mocha Cake

Calories: 265 | Fat: 23.5g | Protein: 9g | Fiber: 3.5g | **Net Carbs: 4g**

This rich cake has all of the flavors of a double mocha espresso latte type thing that you would drink for the same amount of calories but with one major advantage... it's cake, and cake always wins!

SHOPPING LIST

Vegetable oil spray

5 large eggs

1 tablespoon vanilla extract

2 ½ cups almond flour

¾ cup bulk sugar substitute (recommended: Splenda)

¼ cup unsweetened cocoa powder

2 teaspoons dry instant coffee

1 tablespoon baking powder

¼ cup finely chopped hazelnuts, optional

MOCHA BUTTERCREAM FROSTING

4 tablespoons butter, softened

8 ounces cream cheese, softened

1 cup bulk sugar substitute

1 teaspoon instant coffee powder

3 tablespoons unsweetened cocoa powder

1 teaspoon vanilla extract

HELPFUL HINTS

We like to slice the cake horizontally into two layers and frost in between the layers as well.

1 PLACE oven rack in the center position and preheat to 350°F. Spray an 8-inch round cake pan with vegetable oil spray.

2 IN a large bowl, beat eggs until frothy. Add the vanilla extract and ¼ cup of tap water to the bowl, beating to combine.

3 IN another bowl, mix together the almond flour, sugar substitute, cocoa powder, instant coffee, and baking powder.

4 BEAT the dry ingredient mixture into the egg mixture until all is combined.

5 POUR the finished batter into the prepared cake pan and bake 30 to 35 minutes, or until the center is firm and springy and a toothpick inserted into it comes out mostly clean.

6 COOL on a wire rack for 30 minutes before refrigerating at least 2 hours. Turn pan upside down and shake to release the cake.

7 IN an electric mixer on high, whip together all Frosting ingredients until fluffy. Spread evenly across the entire surface of the cake. Sprinkle frosted cake with chopped hazelnuts, if desired.

DESSERTS

Fresh Fruit Pizza

Calories: 305 | Fat: 28g | Protein: 7g | Fiber: 2.5g | **Net Carbs: 5g**

Almonds, eggs, butter, cream cheese, and strawberries are basic staples for a low carb lifestyle that everyone should have on hand at all times. When combined in this recipe, they make one of the most decadent, low carb "legal", and satisfying desserts in our arsenal of cravings busters!

SHOPPING LIST

NUT CRUST

2 ½ cups almond flour

½ cup bulk sugar substitute (recommended: Splenda)

8 tablespoons butter, melted and warm

CREAM CHEESE FILLING

16 ounces cream cheese, softened

1 ½ teaspoons vanilla extract

1 large egg, beaten until frothy

TOPPINGS

2 cups strawberries, hulled and sliced

1 Kiwi, peeled and sliced

HELPFUL HINTS

This pizza may be topped with almost any of your favorite in-season fruits such as blackberries, blueberries, raspberries, peaches, pears, or even figs.

1 PREHEAT oven to 350°F and line a 12-inch pizza pan with parchment paper.

2 IN a large bowl, combine the crust ingredients, mixing well.

3 WHILE crust mixture is still warm from the butter, spoon it onto the lined pan and use a piece of plastic wrap to press it evenly over the bottom. Discard the wrap and bake crust 12 minutes, until lightly browned. Remove and let cool 30 minutes.

4 MEANWHILE, make the filling by whisking together all filling ingredients.

5 USING a spatula, frost the cooled crust with the filling like a cake. Bake 15 minutes at 350°F.

6 REMOVE from oven and decorate the warm pizza with the sliced fruit toppings, pushing each piece down slightly to stick.

7 CHILL pizza in the fridge for a minimum of 3 hours (or the crust may not hold together) before slicing into 12 thin slices.

DESSERTS

ABOUT THE AUTHOR

George Stella has been a professional chef for nearly 30 years. He has appeared on numerous television and news shows, including two seasons of his own show, *Low Carb and Lovin' It*, on the *Food Network*. Most recently he appeared on *The Dr. Oz Show* with his family for a profile on the comfort foods the Stella family reinvented using unique and low carb alternatives to white flour and sugar.

Connecticut born, George has spent more than half of his life in Florida where he lives today with his wife Rachel. This is his fifth cookbook. His first cookbook, *George Stella's Livin' Low Carb* (to which this book is the spiritual successor), is highly regarded as one of the best low carb cookbooks ever written.

To keep up to date on George, please visit:

www.StellaStyle.com

ABOUT THE BOOK

The food photographs and design of this book were done by **Christian and Elise Stella**, George's son and daughter-in-law. They have worked previously on the design and photography of over a dozen cookbooks, most recently Bob Warden's *Great Food Fast*.

All food in the photographs was purchased at an ordinary grocery store or grown in Rachel's garden and prepared exactly to the recipe's directions. All food was prepared by either George or Rachel Stella. No artificial food styling techniques were used to "enhance" the food's appearance. No food prepared for photographs went to waste. The photographs were taken in the Stella home and the home of our family friends and publishers Mary Beth and Michael Guard.

RECIPE INDEX

RECIPE INDEX CONTINUED